JAPANESE THEATRE

Thomas Immoos

JAPANESE THEATRE

Photographs Fred Mayer

English translation Hugh Young

Studio Vista London

A Studio Vista book published by
Cassell & Collier Macmillan Publishers Ltd,
35 Red Lion Square, London WC1R 4SG
and at Sydney, Auckland, Johannesburg,
an affiliate of
Macmillan Publishing Co., Inc.,
New York

Copyright © U. Bär Verlag, Zurich. 1974
Translation copyright © Studio Vista 1977

ISBN 0 289 70802 8

Printed in Switzerland
by Vontobel-Druck AG, Feldmeilen ZH

Contents

Every manifestation of religious or artistic drama, from the simulation dances of the Ice Age hunters in the Ariège caves to Beckett's Theatre of the Absurd and the experiments of the Living Theatre, has made its way to Japan. And the achievement of the Japanese in the field of the theatre compares with the greatest in the world. Noh, Bunraku and Kabuki have long attracted the attention of Western scholars, but very little attempt has been made to describe the Japanese theatre as a whole. Only such a comprehensive approach, following up the fundamental thought and archetypal forms in their historical evolution, can make clear the true meaning of many of the conventions, customs, themes, and motifs. A diachronous analysis is made easier by the fact that all the synchronous forms—that is, the forms as they survive today—are accessible for research.

Among the Japanese, fascinated by the new though they are, the past still looms over the present with an extraordinary power. The theatre is the living archive of the myth, religion and history of Japan. In it the Japanese recognizes himself and his past.

Tokyo 1974   Thomas Immoos

6

PRINCIPLES

Japan

The two first gods, Izanami and Izanagi, stood on the seven-hued rainbow that joins heaven and earth and looked down on the waters of the ocean, flowing into the infinite. The first father dipped his shining sunspear into the water. Pearls fell from the tip of it, drawing a trail of light through the flood, and from them the countless islands of the Japanese kingdom were made. Barren tundra beneath the icy breath of the Siberian storms; tropical luxuriance, whipped by monsoon rains, beaten down by typhoons; golden sand bordering the far-flung bays, and out of the billowing forest the clear silhouette of the perfect mountain; steaming rice fields; stunted pine trees on the steep rocks; a beautiful land, mists that softly veil and seem to reveal the divine. But this island kingdom is constantly threatened by dark forces: the earth quakes under foot, tidal waves break over the shore, the lock gates of heaven are broken, fierce waters burst all the dams. Fiery magma gushes forth from the lap of the earth.

Japan shelters from the giant land masses of the Eurasian continent in a wide curve, the northernmost of the countless islands that inhabit the Pacific Ocean, distant enough to foil the plans of conquerors, near enough for friendly trade and traffic. Here all roads, by water and by land, came to their end.

Old legends tell of an earthly paradise springing from the waves of the eastern sea, where every day a shining sun rose on its course across the sky. For thousands of years people sought these distant islands: the ocean voyagers of the South Seas in their pirogues, patient rice farmers from the monsoon lands, dedicated to the service of Mother Earth under the rule of stern womenfolk, Ice Age hunters from the tundra bound in worship to the beasts they slew, mounted swordsmen from the steppes of Asia who buried their princes in huge barrows.

All brought their cults and their customs with them, and since this was a country where the achievements of human culture were endlessly threat-

ened by the hostile elements, there developed an extraordinary tough-
ness in the preservation of those usages.

Western culture is strictly ruled by the chopping and changing of fashion. New forms and ideas are eagerly taken up and tried out for fertility.
They are played with, experimented with. Sons oppose their fathers,
working on the heritage handed down to them—they elevate, exaggerate
or refine it. Once a style is exhausted and its potential exhausted, it is
given up altogether; there is a break in fashion.

Japanese culture is that of the poor man who has never learned to give
anything up, however eagerly he may grasp at anything new. All styles
are preserved here with an incredible faithfulness. The younger generation displays its loyalty to its heritage by meticulous observance of the
forms it has inherited. Thus, even in the course of hundreds of years,
only small variations creep in. The idea, the concept, the logos, may well
evaporate. But the form remains, in petrified majesty.

The Noh dancer masters a grammar of the dance that embraces no fewer
than three hundred forms *(kata)*. It would be idle to ask what he
thought about that. What he knows is that, over the past five centuries,
his ancestors brought the flower of their art to blossom in the perfection
of this world of form, and that for him too there is no other road to
maturity open.

Since the earliest times the Japanese have shown themselves to be pragmatic; trade has always been more important to them than thinking.
Their ancient religion has no dogma, no ethic; it is just a way to be
followed, the way of the god Shinto, the divine way that, from year to
year, unites gods, ancestral spirits and humans in the glow of the festival
under the sacred trees of the grove before the shrine. Most of all, the
divine way means to them *kagura*: dancing and playing to please the
gods, to teach the people, in magical simulation, prayer and praise.
From the magic and mythical dance there has grown up the colourful,
complex art of the Japanese theatre.

Richard Southern, the English theatrical historian, distinguishes seven
ages of the theatre (*The Seven Ages of the Theatre,* London 1964) and
assumes that these phases follow one another at different times in different cultures. In the West he can only infer the early phases from a few
surviving fossils. In Japan all seven phases can be observed simul-

10

taneously in a living interdependence of functions. The visitor need never go beyond the outskirts of the biggest city in the world to see every theatrical form from prehistoric magic rituals to the most startling 'happening' and the most *avant-garde* underground performance. Japan is a museum of theatrical and religious history.

In the first phase the actor comes on in disguise, playing his role in costume and mask; a nature demon, a ghost, a totem-animal or a god. He has no scenery or properties, no more than he can carry on his body or in his hands. At New Year men disguised as demons, called Namahage, go round the snow-bound villages of northern Japan; they are said to punish naughty children and to drive out sickness. In Tokyo, and in many other places, a lion-dancer goes from house to house to bring good luck.

The second phase brings these performances within the framework of the religious festival. In the open air before the temple the players perform the sacred act—the magic rite, or the telling of mythical tales in which gods and men are firmly linked by fate. By now they have discovered the advantages of a raised stage and an auditorium fitted with seats. There are eighty thousand Shinto shrines scattered over the islands; each village has its own tutelary god and assembles several times a year to invoke his favour with sacrifices, dances and plays. The young men of the village are given responsibility for the religious plays.

In the third phase drama is separated from ritual. The artistic component becomes more important, so the way is opened to the professional actor. Performances now take place inside the houses or palaces. In Japan this step came in the time of Zeami, when Noh ceased to be a religious play and became an amusement of the aristocratic warrior class.

In the fourth phase the professional actors turn their attention to the development of the stage facilities, to provide a serviceable instrument for their steadily improving art. The Noh stage, with its typical division into three—playing area, bridge *(hashigakari)* and dressing room— reveals its descent from the temple plays. It is still often located in the open, and—like Shakespeare's stage—dispenses with scenery.

In the fifth phase we find experiments with décor. To protect these expensive adjuncts from the elements, and to get better lighting effects, it is now necessary to move into a covered theatre. In Japan this step was taken by Kabuki in the eighteenth century.

In the sixth phase the theatre develops all the newly acquired facilities of the theatre of illusion, with the large-scale use of scenery, costume and stage techniques. Kabuki developed the revolving stage and trapdoor quite early, and can still captivate the most hardened spectator with the magic of its décor and the speed with which scenes are changed.

In the seventh phase the theatre rebels against the rule of the machine and regains a new artistic freedom, renouncing illusion, identification and transformation through the 'alienation' approach of the Brechtian, anti-Aristotelian theatre. The modern theatre is still slightly hesitant about taking this path, but underground groups have committed themselves to it unreservedly.

Magic

I will dance that dance, that makes to turn the towers of the moon.

(Hagoromo)

The first experience of early man:

The process of life flows ceaselessly to and fro between two poles. Each morning the sun rises, shining, on its daily round. The bright sky is its kingdom, the energy of productive man its symbol. Beneath its gleaming touch all life flowers. But every evening, when it sets, it dies away.

Then the rule of night begins. The dark earth, kingdom of sleep and of death, is allied to night. Its symbol is the mother in labour, the mysterious essence of womanhood.

The year too runs its course in an ever-repeated cycle of germination, flowering, ripeness and death. The same cycle is repeated in the growth and decay of man, in the alternation of birth and death.

Nature and man are subject to the same cosmic decrees. Their life processes are passed in the same rhythms; they appoint the times of days, years and lives. In the tension, the interchange, the flow of these life forces hither and thither, the cosmic terms are also ceaselessly fulfilled. It was only in very recent times that ethical values, the concept of good and evil, were imputed to them. In the beginning, as in oriental thought, they were without such values.

A fine-spun network of secret forces and influences surrounds and permeates the universe. The fate of man is largely decided by the interplay of this relationship.

Through a mystic partnership man can bring his own actions to bear on the system of cosmic forces. The medium of this partnership is a powerful, all-controlling fluid called *mana*. For the prosperity of man and the ordered progression of the cosmos it is essential that he inserts the right actions into this network of complex agreements.

Mana is particularly concentrated in certain people: in midwives, in spiritually inspired shaman women, in magicians and yogis. To them is

13

given the power to influence the course of the cosmic processes. This power comes to them through a special gift, by spiritual concentration or by the practice of potent rites and usages. It was from the performance of these that the first theatre was born. Religion, magic, myth and art are inextricably woven together in it.

Early man was not a philosopher but a man of action. Before he made his needs known to the celestial powers by words, by prayers, he described to them what it was he wanted. This age-old talent gave birth to drama, *dromenon* in the literal sense, something performed that is described by actions (δράω = to do). Originally this *dromenon* was wholly incorporated in the performance of the rite. The ritual expresses deeply felt sentiments and desires through symbolic representation of the objects or events desired. The rites include, not only the speaking of a prayer, but also magic simulation; they bring about what they describe—the return of the life-giving sun after the long winter nights, the longed-for rain with its mighty accompaniment of the dreaded lightning, the new growth of vegetation from the dead rigor of winter.

The dancer possessed of *mana* stands at the centre of the universe. Through the rhythmic circling of his dance he keeps the course of the stars in motion, drives the sun and moon on their way, calls down rain, makes seeds sprout and fruit ripen. The Japanese word for dance is *mai*, which is derived from *mau* = to turn.

In the rhythmic circling, driven on by the regular beat of drums and cymbals and flowing melodies on the flute, the dancer gradually falls into a trance. The rhythm and melody are too strong for him; his will is exhausted. 'The movements are performed as if by themselves, with no personal effort. Personal consciousness completely fades out and is lost in unconsciousness' (D. Günther). The soul is freed from its link with the body; the unconquerable delight of complete freedom of movement, rising up from the depth of the unconscious, free from earthly heaviness, blessed by an enhanced sensation of life.

Intoxicated by the rhythmic circling and swinging, the dancer experiences a feeling of liberation, of release from the fetters of personality; he enters into a wide-reaching communion with his fellow dancers and with the whole clan. He is beside himself in the full sense of the words. The circle grows wider. The elements are taken in, water and

14

wind join in, plants and trees, tame animals and wild animals, the stars in heaven, all join in the all-embracing dance. The walls collapse between the things of this world and the things of the beyond. Supernatural beings, elemental spirits, angels and gods draw trails of light as they dance.

The dancer is of the ancient tribe of Orpheus and the even older tribe of the shamans, they who by the power of music, of song and dance, keep the universe moving on its course. At the golden sounds spun by the lyre, rocks melt away, wild beasts are tamed, that first paradisial state in which man comprehends the speech of plants and animals gently draws near. Pythagoras, son of Apollo, god of song, knew that heaven is the home of music. Earthly melodies are but imitations of heavenly music, of the harmony of the spheres from the divine, blessed cosmos. However deaf the blunted ears of earthly beings may be to these harmonies, Pythagoras could still hear them, and used their magic power to tame a wild bear (Van der Waerden). What the first dancers unconsciously performed, what the myth prophetically told, is raised into bright consciousness by the poets and dancers of Noh.

In *Hagoromo (The Robe of Feathers)*, Zeami tells the story, familiar all over the world, of the descent of the swan-maiden. The form of this play is very ancient; the story, hardly more than a sketch, offers little more than an opportunity to praise the wonders of natural beauty in a set of splendid dances, to make known the cosmic function of the dance and foreshadow the glory of the supernatural world. In the pine wood on the shore, with the sacred mountain Fuji rising in its majesty above it, a fisherman finds a robe of feathers hanging on a pine tree. Then the swan-maiden appears, wearing the golden crown always worn by celestial sends down fortune and prosperity to the land of mortals:

ing a bathe in the cool waters. She may not return to the Elysian fields without her feather robe. She is a flightless bird, she laments, looking up to the way through the clouds with vain longing. Her sorrow moves the fisherman, and he gives her back the robe of feathers on condition that she will show him the dances that are danced in heaven. Deeply grateful, she dances for him the dance of the rainbow skirt and the dance of the robe of feathers, then the dance 'that makes to turn the towers of the moon':

15

                  Fairy: This is the Palace of the Moon,
                          Built with a jade axe
                          For everlasting time.
                Chorus: Fairies from heaven dressed in white,
                          Fairies from heaven dressed in black,
                          Three times five as the moon waxes,
                          Three times five as the moon wanes,
                          That is the number of them.
                          One heavenly lady serves
                          Every moonlit night.

The real service of the heavenly ladies in the moon god's palace, their cosmic dance, is to keep the stars in motion from day to day. The last chorus expresses gratitude again that the dance of the heavenly ladies sends down fortune and prosperity to the land of mortals:

                          Buddha's promises are fulfilled,
                          Our home
                          Gleams with the seven treasures
                          Which this dance rained down upon us,
                          The gifts of heaven.

Tsunemasa, a prince of the house of Taira, is another member of a race with magic musical powers. Since his earliest youth he had found favour with the emperor, who gave him a costly lute. When he died in battle this was offered to a temple as a sacrifice for the rest of its owner's soul. Flute and string music are joined with the prayers of the monks. Suddenly, in the flickering torchlight, the shade of the dead man appears, conjured up by the prayers and the music. With the dry sound of their plectrums the chorus recalls the vow of Benten, goddess of music, to lead all beings to redemption through the heavenly music of the lute.

The dead man had been an example of every virtue, but he had earned special praise in his lifetime by his full accord with nature. He had found his pleasure,

                          Evermore by birds and flowers,
                          By wind and moonlight,
                          To write poems

16

And to sing songs
To the harmonies of flutes and lute.
Thus he spent each spring and autumn.

As the singing and playing of the liturgy proceeds, the strings of the sacrificial lute suddenly, magically, begin to hum, touched by the dead hand of their master, still invisible in the flickering of the torches. It is elemental music, the music of the spheres, that sounds in his melody. Full of wonder, the chorus describes it with quotations from Chinese poets.

Tsunemasa: At the edge of the clouds
The moon hangs bright
Over the pine trees of the mountain range.
Chorus: It is the wind you hear.
The wind, soughing through the pine woods
Like the patter of rain in winter.
O sublime hour!
The deep strings droned and moaned,
Like the patter of rain in winter.
And the high strings whispered secretly,
The first string and the second
Rustled like wind through the pine-needles.
The third and the fourth strings
Wailed like a caged crane,
Calling to its young in the night,
In soft, whimpering tones.

Then Tsunemasa sings a Chinese song; he knows well the cosmic effects of his music:
One note of the bamboo mouth-organ
Drives away
Autumn clouds from the hill slopes.

In this piece the music and prayers can only conjure up the dead man from the kingdom of the shadows for one night. At first light the hate and anger that he felt for his enemies seize him again and drag him back into the dark night of the demons. Because he still harbours dark feelings of revenge, he may not enter into Nirvana.

Perfect redemption through the magic power of song is the theme of the bewitching play of the iris, *Kakitsubata.* A mendicant monk visits the eight bridges of Mikawa, where the irises, hymned by the poet Narihira in his *Legend of Ise,* bloom so gloriously. A village maiden appears, and in dialogue they vow remembrance to the poet. The wanderer shelters in her cabin for the night. The maiden then reveals herself in a shining dress as the spirit of the iris that the poet sang of and loved. She wears the costly Chinese robe, embroidered with patterns of lilies, in which the empress Takeko had once danced in a great festival and captivated the poet's heart. But at the same time she dons the crown and sword that Narihira wore when he first beheld the empress. In the appearance of this iris spirit there are Yin and Yang; in the sacred dance, released from the pain of separation the androgynous being rejoices in age-old unity and fulfilment. They begin to celebrate the memory of the poet; one after another his songs are expressed in the dance. Moon and wind, flower and tree, enter into the song of praise. Through his art of story and song the poet has become the incarnation of the Boddhisatva of music. Whatever he names shares in redemption through his word and becomes a Buddha. Grasses and trees pray to him for the gift of dew.

This is poetry and sacred dance as sacrament, an earthly expression of celestial healing. In his late work *Mirror of the Flowers,* Zeami plumbs the metaphysical depths. 'Dance and song stem from Nyoraizo, their foundation and their source.' Nyorai is the first Buddha, Tathagata; the historical Buddha Shakyamuni and all other Buddhas are later incarnations of him. Nyoraizo is the treasure-house of Tathagata. A quotation from the *Shoman Sutra* may clarify Zeami's difficult thinking: 'The way in which the omnipotent essence of Buddha remains a part of everything that exists, and exists eternally by becoming of similar substance to them, that is something that is truly beyond our understanding. That the presence of the Buddha in everything that exists, though it is true, is hidden in the world of error, that is called Nyoraizo'—that is to say, the treasury of the original Buddha, the hidden, the eternal. In our terminology we might say: dance and song flow from the depth of divinity.

How this divine music breathes through the whole of creation with the ever-present spirit of Buddha is shown by Zeami in *Takasago,* a Noh play often asked for as a mystic play of benediction on festive occasions—at a wedding, for instance. Zeami first quotes a Chinese poem: 'All that is blest or unblest cannot live without song', and then goes on:

> Grass, trees, earth,
> Sighing of the wind
> Babbling of water,
> These myriad things
> Conceal a heart.
> The wood in springtime
> In the east wind,
> The insects in autumn,
> Chirping in the dew:
> In all that is
> Sings a song.

Another play speaks of an endless song that thrills through everything that has life. The drums are the waves, the flute the voice of the dragons in the sea.

This hidden song that sleeps in all things is what the Noh play seeks to bring to life. That is why it is so closely interwoven with nature. Each play has its appropriate season of the year and is normally only performed at that season. Delicate allusions in the text capture the magic of the season. Thus, later, a master of puppet play recitation wrote: 'The technique of the play is learned from the master. But true mastery is learned from flowers, trees, wind and moon.' Holy are the things of nature, mysteriously permeated by the divine essence. The Noh play looses their tongues and gives them solid shape, coloured life, swirling dance. So the spirits of the cherry tree, of the plum, the maple, the willow, the pine tree emerge from their vegetable imprisonment and gain the power of speech to proclaim their destiny and their philosophy. The spirits of irises, wisteria, lilies, peonies, blossom with delicate life in the highest poetic transfiguration. Ancient Japanese animism adopts Buddhist terminology: 'Grasses and trees, the earth itself, all are Buddha', we hear in the play *Black Cherry Flowers*—a play staged only on the death of the emperor.

The praise of springtime is the theme of the play *Kōcho (Butterfly)*. The plum blossom, first messenger of spring, comes out in the ruins of an ancient palace before the spring begins. A wandering monk goes there from the loneliness of the mountains where ascetics submit themselves to severe penances, so that, just once in his life, he may enjoy the sight of the imperial city in the glory of spring. A girl comes out of the deserted building. In the dialogue that follows, the lovely maiden at first sidesteps the question of where she comes from and what she is called. But at last she lifts the veil of her secrecy: she is the ghost of a butterfly. In spring, summer and autumn she flits idly from flower to flower, the friend of all the trees and plants. But there is one flower that she is forbidden to visit. It opens while the winter wind is still icy—the plum blossom. Every year, before the coming of spring, she sheds tears for it. She knows about the dream of Juang-ze who thought he was a butterfly, or a butterfly that thought it was Juang-ze. Vanity of vanity! In the same palace the prince Genji the Magnificent, hero of the great love romances, once held his revels. Then Bugaku dancers in splendid robes dance the butterfly dance; but everything vanishes as in a dream. The monk and his companion pass the night under a tree, reciting the *Lotus Sutra* for the happiness of butterflies. In their sleep the butterfly appears to them filled with joy. It has been saved by their prayers; it is no longer to be parted from the plum blossom. Happily it dances the butterfly dance for them:

Drawn wondrously by the power of prayer,
All division vanishes between men and flowers.
The flowering tree bears fruit of enlightenment.

I am no longer kept away from the plum blossom;
I may hover and flutter about it.

In springtime, in summer, in autumn and in winter
The trees are in blossom.
At the tip of the bough hangs my heart.

From the blossom of the butterfly's dance,
Eddying snowfall;
Arms that circle in the dance, oh so gloriously!

20

It circles fluttering round the petals,
The wheels of the little wagon turn,
And the butterfly draws power of enlightenment from it.

The image of the butterfly in the spring night
Becomes the Boddhisatva of the dance.
The clouds grow clearer in the butterfly's wing-beats.
It departs in the spring mist.

Like from like, like to like—that is the rule that governs the conduct of primitive man. A given set of gestures will always produce a definite, and to that extent a 'like', sequence of actions on the part of the primal forces. It is the set of gestures that activates the powers' desired response, creating order in the cosmic powers and keeping the bi-polar stream of life in proper motion. Not that the Noh dancer has any idea of any such primordial lore; but his dance springs from the same primitive human experience. The Japanese has a long memory; he can freeze old forms, old ideas, and reproduce them unchanged over the centuries. Thus primitive ritual survives in the modern theatre, though its nature and significance are often quite unknown.

This is perhaps the place to consider a subject found throughout cultural and theatrical history: rain magic.

We begin with the meaning of three characters in Chinese writing. Chinese picture-writing not only played an important part in Japanese cultural history in earlier times; it is also, for the intelligent observer, a textbook of religious history of the first order. There are forms contained in it from which we can recognize a shaman culture that spread from central Asia over the whole of eastern Asia.

The Chou peoples, who in proto-historic times—that is, in the second millennium BC—broke out of central Asia into China and built up a powerful kingdom, brought with them the idea of a god in heaven who ruled over all other gods and spirits. But the good earth was also important, for plant life was constantly renewed from it to feed men and animals. Man stands between the male heaven and the female earth. He too is divided into two sexes; by appropriate action he can control the mysterious working of the cosmic powers, so that the life process can run its course without interruption.

This concept is represented by the character 工. The upper line stands for heaven, the lower for earth. The vertical line in between stands for mankind, the mid-point of the cosmic framework, who connects both poles through his magic actions, 'doing' in the highest sense of the word. So the character gets the sense of 'doing'; today it means particularly the work of the carpenter.

The second character 巫 takes these ideas a stage further. Until recent times the shamans of Siberia used to practise a rite giving symbolical expression to this philosophy: an arrow was stuck vertically in the ground and a plank laid horizontally across it to symbolize heaven. The shamans then danced in a circle round this device, which stood for the first character—the primal dance that represents the sun's orbit, the passing of the year, the rotation of the stars. The second character 巫 actually represents this ceremony: two men—shamans—dancing round the cosmic symbol and so carrying out their magic 'doing'. This sign was already known on oracle-bones in ancient China. Oracle-bones are the oldest written monuments ever discovered, dating from the second millennium BC. In Chinese the character has the meaning of shamans on whom an intelligent spirit, Shen, has descended; it particularly stands for females. Important functions in the arrangements for funerals are entrusted to them: determination of the order of priority of the gods and ancestral spirits called to the festivities, the proper order of the sacrifices, choice of the right instruments and clothing, colours and tunes, the selection of which depended on the season of the year. Especially they had to call up the gods or spirits to themselves by ecstatic dances, to lend their own bodies to them and express by mime in the dance what the god wanted to say to them. They were dressed for the occasion in fine white robes, and carried a flower in their hands. As we can now see, this was a primitive form of the *kagura* (shrine dance) which still forms an essential part of the Shinto liturgy. The second character described above is read in Japanese as *miko*, and stands for the sacred dancing-girls who serve in the biggest temples as well as for the shaman women who officiate all over the country to pray for good health, to call up the dead, and as oracles. Kurozawa Akira's film *Rasho-*

22

mon included an extraordinarily impressive sequence in which a *miko* called up the spirit of the murdered samurai and lent him her voice so that he could give the court his version of the murder scene. No one could fail to be reminded of the witch of Endor, who at Saul's command called up Samuel from the underworld (1 Sam. 28:8–25).

The third character takes these ideas further still: 靈. We can find on oracle-bones the sign for a cloud, which has drops of water on it, 靁, and beneath it, three times, the sign for an open mouth. This obviously represents a prayer for rain, uttered with open mouth and with great intensity (hence the triple repetition of the open mouth). This ancient character is only used in modern script in combination with the second character 巫 (*miko*). Its meaning is easily read: two shaman women dancing round the cosmic symbol (heaven, man, earth) and raising their voices in a prayer for rain.

Such magic rain dances, round in circles to the accompaniment of drums and cymbals to represent thunder and lightning, are still widespread in Japan. A few years ago the government radio service broadcast one of them when a long drought was causing a very serious water shortage in the capital at the hottest time of the year. That very night the longed-for rain fell at last. The postman, the milkman, the taxi-driver were all quite sure that the dance was responsible.

The simple man in Japan has never displayed any tendency towards abstract thinking. Action has always been more important to him than losing himself in metaphysical speculation. Nor has he ever been at all interested in obscure abstract symbolism. So his ritual is elementary—carried out, that is, on the basis of his actual experience of the elements and on the familiar, well established lines.

There is a shrine in northern Japan (Kitafukuoka, in the Iwate prefecture) where there is a well three metres (ten feet) deep which gives very clear, pure, cold water. (As proof of its exceptional quality, a saké factory takes it away in tankers; the quality of rice wine depends very much on the water used.) The still, crystalline pool mirrors huge trees in which the gods dwell, and out of it, from mysterious sources, the life-enhancing element flows endlessly. The sacred place is instinct with divinity. At such places natural things become transparent: the beyond, the supernatural can be seen, sensed. When the area is threatened by drought the

23

priest puts on the lion-mask, which is worshipped in the temple as sacred. To the sound of drums, flutes and cymbals he dances with it round the crystal spring, then dives into the cool waters to make quite clear to the god that dwells in the mask what it is he wants from him.

In many places they carry the lion-mask, or a statue of Buddha, a bell or a puppet in ceremonial procession to a river or pool to wash them. Rain magic dances are always accompanied by the rhythm of drums and cymbals, which represent the fecundating thunder and lightning. The prayers and rites are directed to the appropriate deities of rain and water: the god of thunder, the dragon king, Bishamon, the water goddess, and so on.

It is a long way from such present-day ceremonies back to the archaic ritual that we can still recognize from the Chinese characters. For thousands of years the way lies through the dark. Here and there occasional flashes of light appear in historic documents, but they illumine only the ceremonial dances and plays performed at the imperial court and in the great shrines and temples. For the simple people, history affords us only a long, deep silence.

Some scholars think that the dance rites of shaman women on the continent of Asia may be the origin of *Gosechi-no-mai,* the dance that the daughters of the most distinguished families performed before the emperor on the occasion of the great banquets held during harvest festivals. Four or five carefully selected dancers, in magnificent white robes with long, dangling sleeves which they rotate with a fluttering motion, circle the stage five times. (The empress herself led this dance when Narihira was captivated by the sight of her; see above.) Legend tells us about the origin of this dance. The emperor Temmu went on a journey to the Yoshiro river, where he played on a five-stringed Korean *koto* (zither). The magic sounds tempted some heavenly maidens down to earth; they danced before the emperor and sang songs in five parts, and their sleeves fluttered like whirling snow. Each one had her own kind of dance, and when they danced together it made the beholder think of spirits dancing above the clouds.

The fivefold arm movements and the form of the zither point to Korea, the white clothing and circling of the stage to the customs of the shaman women. This court dance is reckoned to be the original form of the

24

fertility dances that later developed to such a great extent in connexion with the planting and harvesting of rice, and that, by way of Dengaku, led to Noh. It may be that we have here the direct link connecting the original dance of the shaman women of central Asia with Japan, though of course the true basic patterns are no longer so easy to grasp.

The Bugaku repertory today includes two dances, *Somakusha* and *Soshimari,* in which the dancers wear straw raincoats; the latter is particularly impressive, because it makes the god of thunder, Susano-o, the wild brother of the sun goddess Amaterasu, appear from Izumo. Still having simulation magic in mind, we are justified in assuming that here too we have something that derives originally from the performances of the rain magicians. The oldest courtly art in the world, still practised today, has been transformed by a thousand-year-long process of stylization into pure abstraction. The practical symbolism has long since evaporated.

With the Noh play, however, we are on surer ground. The magic performed by the peasants through thousands of years of unrecorded darkness, the myths and usages that flowed into Japan from every country of Asia, here become formalized; the magic powers of the shamans, the mystic experience of the Taoists, the divination of the wizards using the oracle of Yin and Yang—it is all concentrated in the religious ceremonies of the great shrines and takes shape as a mystery play, as a service of benediction, as the potent ritual of simulation.

The play *Ema—the horse image* is a good example. Long ago it was the custom to sacrifice a black horse to the gods when rain was needed, but a white horse if too much rain had fallen and the people wanted the sun to shine. There is very little animal sacrifice in Shinto; the custom probably originated on the continent of Asia. The sacrifice of animals was forbidden under Buddhist influence, in about A.D. 791. Such sacrifices have only been kept up into present times in a few places: they still sacrifice goats in Suwa and hares in Chiba. (Sea creatures were not included under the ban.) The horse was a late arrival in the island kingdom, introduced by those riders from the steppes who in proto-historic times brought an aristocratic warrior culture to Japan, burying their princes in enormous barrows. The little, shaggy steppe pony must have been particularly precious to them, as we can tell from the expensively accoutred clay figures, *haniwa,* that surrounded the princes' burial places. In sacrificing a horse these people must have been offering what they held most dear. Later on they substituted a votive image for the living animal. On New Year's Eve unseen hands would bring a white or black figure of a horse into the temple, and this oracle determined whether sun or rain would dominate in the coming year.

The imperial messenger appears in the shrine of the sun goddess in Ise to pray for the right proportion of rain and sunshine for the whole kingdom in the new year. A specially chosen bridal couple praises the shrine and its theophanies; they hang up in the antechamber a white and a black image of a horse. The myth of the shrine is told in dialogue and dance. Then the divinities themselves appear and perform the cosmic dance. The dance of the gods is always a special climax in a mystery play.

There is a present-day custom linked with this rain magic; on New Year's Eve the emperor offers a sacrifice of white and black saké (rice wine) in the palace sanctuary.

The Indian play *Solitary Unicorn* stages the rain magic in exotic dress. By dint of severe discipline, an ascetic has gained supernatural powers—he is one of the world of yogis and Taoist genii who can work magic. One day he slips on some stones made wet by the rain, and breaks his water-jug. Furious, he shuts up the dragon king, who governs the rain, in a cave in the rocks. For long months not a drop of rain falls; drought threatens, a ruined harvest, starvation. Sages and dignitaries take counsel with the emperor to determine how the floodgates of the heavens may be opened. A courtier advises them to choose the loveliest of the three thousand ladies in waiting, so that she may seduce the hermit and deprive him of his magic powers. The lovely Shenta, with five hundred servant-girls, goes out before his cell. The beautiful girls dance and sing and feast on the best food and drink. They manage to get the hermit to join them in their merrymaking and feasting. The hermit is intoxicated and moved to passion—and thereupon he loses his magic powers. A roar comes from the cave:

    Chorus: The mountain wind comes down
            With a wild roar.
            The sky grows dark.
            The cave trembles.

Mighty rocks crash down.
The dragon king appears.
The hermit sees him,
Attacks him with the sharpness of the sword,
Girt with the armour of wrath,
Swinging the devilish sword,
He battles with the dragon.
But his magic power is forfeit.
His powers fade.
At last he lies stretched on the ground.
The dragon king thrusts
Joyfully through the dark clouds.
Lightning and thunder fill
The floodgates of the heavens,
Heavy rain hammers down.
The great rivers are saved.
Over the white-foaming waves,
The prancing waves,
He hastens homeward
To the dragon-city below the sea.

This subject, under the title *Narukami,* found a place in the canon of the eighteen representative Kabuki plays for the performance of which Danjuro VII (1791–1859) gave his family exclusive rights. The play was first staged by Danjuro I in 1684. The fable is exotic, not native to Japan; nowadays the erotic motifs are greatly extended to make a strange mixture of Buddhist asceticism and lighthearted sex. The original significance of the rain magic is totally forgotten. Kabuki never minds about a touch of the titillating and vulgar.

The hermit Narukami had brought a petition to the emperor, but had not been heard. In revenge he resorts to magic, and imprisons the rain god in a stone-walled pool below a waterfall. No more rain falls to refresh the thirsty fields. The imperial princess Taema-Hime is ready to sacrifice herself; she sets off for the mountain cell to rob the hermit of his magic powers by her seductive charms.

Two monks hold her back from the cell. Women are not allowed to enter it. She makes them listen to her by telling them her tragic love story.

Even the hermit, who is sunk in prayer nearby, begins to listen to her, and allows her into his cell. Her story so excites him that he swoons. By tender womanly arts she is able to restore him to consciousness. Suddenly she complains of severe pains. The hermit tells her that he is a doctor and can heal by the laying on of hands. It is the first time he has ever touched a woman's body. Gropingly he explores her anatomy, commenting on his discoveries with scraps from the Buddhist anthropology. The fires of passion begin to burn in him; her beauty and his passion rob him of his wits. 'I am undone. I am going down into hell. But my happiness is there.' At this moment of supreme pleasure he is transformed into a demon. His white ascetic's robe changes in an instant into a robe of fire. His powers are gone. The princess cuts the sacred straw rope that sanctifies his home and keeps the dragon king imprisoned. The rain falls. This mixture of magic, corrupt Buddhism and vulgar eroticism, a vehicle for all the stagecraft of Kabuki, provided an ideal part for a great actor.

Even in the Bunraku puppet theatre there were plays that could be used as rain magic. In 1724 a long drought visited the region of Awa and the island of Awaji, where Bunraku was first established and performed. Prayers for rain were offered in all the temples and shrines, but with no result. Then the prince of the region ordered the Uemara troupe to put on a rain magic play in the temple of the war god Hachiman. The master himself took part—and behold, it rained heavily for twelve days.

The same thing happened in 1794. First prayers were offered, day and night, without bringing a single drop of rain. Then the prince of the region ordered the puppet players to act the Noh ritual of *Okina (The Old Man)*, which for more than a thousand years has been used as the most important of the mysteries of benediction. The players performed the service for seventeen days, and on ten days it rained.

An old puppet player whose memory goes back to the beginning of this century tells how a play by Chikamatsu Monzaemon was used as rain magic in those days. The play was dedicated to the tragic hero Sugawara-no-Michizane: *The Story of the Sky God Sugawara*. Sugawara is numbered among the greatest heroes of Japanese history: a master of the poet's art, an outstanding student of Chinese wisdom and scholarship, a true servant of his lord, the last statesman to try to maintain his

28

emperor's complete power against the almighty tribe of the imperial administration, Fujiwara. His heroism is ill rewarded: he is deprived of all state offices and banished to remote Kyushu, where he pines away in sorrow and longing for the imperial court and soon sinks into the grave. But then he is changed into the sky god, to destroy his enemies with thunder and lightning. The Noh play *Raiden (Thunder and Lightning)* describes how he appears on earth in a downpour of rain and is created god of the sky by the emperor. This Noh play too may sometimes be used as rain magic. From the Kabuki version, which has a highly complicated plot, only one short scene, lasting about thirty minutes, is used as rain magic. Michizane is banished to Kyushu through the intrigues of his enemies. But they do not cease to persecute him, until at last he is murdered. The hero is transformed into the god of lightning and strikes his enemies down. Then he ascends into heaven. His disciple follows after him, but the steep rocky walls prevent him from advancing further. He commits ritual suicide, as many real samurai did in their desire to follow their lord even into the kingdom of the dead. He too is changed into a lightning flash, and shakes heaven and earth. His blood fertilizes the flowers of the rice field.

An old actor who used to take part in this play tells with pride how, even before he got home after the performance, the sky would have grown dark and stormy rain would have begun to fall. This magic was often performed when he was young, and always had the desired result. The basic idea of the ritual has remained the same for three thousand years; it has simply been expressed through different media in different ways. Frozen time.

Myth

The background to the Noh stage, the one, invariable scene, is a painting of a vast, gnarled pine tree. The original of this tree still stands in the broad park that surrounds the Kasuga shrine in Nara. It is called Yogo-matsu, the tree which the shades bid welcome.

In ancient times, before the Japanese had learned from the Chinese the art of building temples, they believed, like the Germans and the Celts, that the gods lived in huge trees. They performed their sacrifices before such trees in the sacred groves. But from the earliest times the highest form of sacrifice has always been the dance, the liturgical mystery play. These religious dances are rooted deep in the traditions of the myth. In mythical times the supernatural powers approached much nearer than they did according to the magic view of life. An intimate relationship with them is within reach of anyone who can learn how to establish it; stories in the legends and the mimetic dances tell both of their own remote life and of their association with mortals.

What does the Japanese mean when he uses the word *kami*, which we generally translate as god, gods, divinities? Certainly not anything eternal, transcendental, or even absolute, existing by itself. Gods are supernatural beings from a variety of origins—through the apotheosis of raised-up ancestral spirits, religious heroes, war heroes, representatives of the national history and aspirations; but they also personify the religious animation of the world. In every object, in every sphere, every phenomenon in nature there dwells and works something holy—holy in the sense of the Latin word *sacer*, which can stand at the same time for both consecration and execration. The fantasy behind the myths makes itself images of this divine presence in nature and surrounds them with an aura of authenticity that gives them a destiny, a history. This is exactly what myth means—the telling of a story. Gods are beings that can both bless and threaten. The Japanese myth distinguishes between *kami*, who mainly, if not entirely, represent the kindly, beneficent side of nature, and *oni*, demons, which appear as threatening, dangerous, sinister spirits. It is man's most urgent task to ensure the favour of the supernatural world and protect himself against its displeasure. The gods are both distant and near.

The veil can be lifted on either side, the natural forms become transparent and the supernatural reality, great and shining or terrible and menacing, comes forth out of the objects it dwells in.

> O gods, gods!
> You oft-appearing sleepers in all things,
> Who rise up joyfully.
>
> (Rilke)

A substantial proportion of Noh plays, especially though not exclusively the god-plays, have just this form of theophany as their subject. It is not only the gods of particular shrines that appear at the celebration of their festivals; nature spirits also suddenly emerge from things. The spirit of the cherry blossom blames the monk Saigyo for thinking too selfishly of meditative rest and denying visitors access to the wonder of the blossom. Flower spirits, water sprites, mountain fairies assume shape and speech. They are always there, close to mankind, but at the same time far off in inaccessible remoteness, for the eyes of mortals are limited so that they are not always aware of this presence. So the supernatural is simultaneously present and absent.

But when the 'festival sun' shines, the gods' remoteness is changed into a gladdening nearness: parousia, epiphany, theophany. The divinity comes from afar, from the remote distance, to the festival place, into the circle of the expectant community. During the festival man experiences the latent presence of the deity in a higher degree of sensibility, which will stay with him in his everyday life. Every shrine celebrates its own *matsuri*. The basic idea is the same everywhere: in the beginning, the god came down from a tree. Later he was transferred from it into the shrine building, where he made his home in some symbol—a stone, perhaps, a branch, a mirror, a mask, a sword. This object is not identified with the god; it would be quite wrong to describe it as a fetish or idol. The god, who in his own nature exists somewhere in the distance, in a kind of transcendence, is at the same time, in a way that we cannot fathom more

32

closely, present also in this object of worship. Modern Christian liturgical scholarship uses the idea of a material symbol to represent the essence of a symbol that also stands for a real presence. The same idea seems to be entirely applicable to a closer understanding of the theological problem posed by Shinto. When the festival is held, this material symbol is carried back to the sacred tree in solemn procession. A temporary shrine or altar will have been built there, and sacrifices, prayers, dances and plays are performed for the god's pleasure.

The festival always takes the same basic form, which in fact underlies every Shinto liturgy:

> *Kami-oroshi:* summoning of the gods or spirits.
> *Kami-asobi:* entertainment of the gods.
> *Kami-agari:* return of the gods.

The summoning: gods and ancestral spirits come to men from distant regions—from the azure depth of the sky, from the peaks of far mountains where the spirits of the dead dwell, out of the foaming waves of the sea. A scene from Okinawa: a rocky peak that falls steeply into the sea; a group of old men and women gather round the base of it, lift their hands in prayer and with loud voices sing prayers and supplications: *kami-uta,* the song of god. The word *uta* is related to the Indonesian word *i'da,* which means magic speech. We may find something in common with Swiss yodelling, the nightly call to prayer over the Alpine meadows that calls down protective spirits and drives off evil ones. The Shinto priest, too, calling on a god, makes a mysterious sound, a vowel sound like *oo,* beginning low in the range of his voice and slowly rising—an ancient sound from religious history, which still grips the hearts of all who hear it. We can see here the beginnings of the slow evolution of sacred music that led to Bach's High Mass.

Anyone who attends a Noh performance for the first time, with mixed fascination and consternation, will probably find nothing more irritating than the extraordinary shouting and calling with which the drummers accompany their rhythms, vocal sounds that begin deep and rise into the highest register, *kakegoe.* Men's voices have taken over the functions of a musical instrument now, but the origin of this custom is prayer, coaxing the gods to descend—the call to prayer, primitive yodelling.

Another way of attracting the gods is calling them by name. The flower festival, *hanamatsuri*, near Nagoya, an ancient New Year ritual, is introduced by the recitation of long lists of gods. But epiclesis, 'the calling of the Name', is also the title given to an important prayer in the liturgy of the Orthodox Church, which according to their doctrine effects the transubstantiation of the bread and wine.

Man is fertile in the invention of ways of attracting the deities. Great fires burn before the shrine in the groves at night to show them the way. Drums beat ceaselessly, flutes shrill powerful rhythms. These are the two traditional shaman instruments; in ancient times drums were fashioned from the skulls of dead men and covered with human skin, and flutes were made from human bones. There are still such things to be found in Tibet; and there are magnets there too, charged with *mana* to attract the spirits. In the dance ritual of the Yamabushi the dancers hold up opened fans or a rod with bells behind the curtain while the music plays—ritual lightning conductors to attract the divine spirit, obvious symbols to the pragmatic Japanese.

The entertainment: when the gods have taken their place on the seat prepared for them the second and most important part of the festival begins, the entertainment for the pleasing of the gods, *kami-asobi*. Offerings of food and drink are brought to them, majestic invocations recited in classical language. But the true offering is the religious dance, which quite often develops into a dramatic mystery play. The religious dance is the true mystery of Shintoism, the precipitate of the Japanese people's age-old religious experiences. It is prayer in dance, sacrifice in dance. In it we can see at once the origins of Japan's rich theatrical art.

Etymologists give more than a dozen different explanations of the word *kagura* (religious dance). Many of them believe the derivation is from *kami-kura* (seat of the gods), while others prefer the interpretation from the present-day pictograph. The latter can be interpreted in two ways, as music and as pleasure or joy, so that the word *kagura* describes the pleasing of the gods by dance and music. Dancing is indeed among the gods' greatest pleasures. Whenever they reveal themselves to men in mystery plays, it is always in the form of a majestic dance. The sky, the whole of creation, is constantly turning in a circular motion, in the dance of the heavenly maidens, of the spirits of the elements and of nature. No wonder they look for no greater pleasure from their festival than the offering of the ritual dance. So this dance liturgy has a peculiar double character; it is a human activity of sacrifice and prayer, calling on the deities for all good gifts, but at the same time it is also a divine activity, the grant of benediction, good luck and prosperity, the miracle of creation, revelation, parousia. It is in the fullest sense *medetashi,* fortunate, full of all that is good. We cannot but think of the Christian sacrament, the earthly symbol that grants heavenly grace.

There is a great range of variations in the spectrum of the meaning, the sense of *kagura.* The picture described earlier of the age-old magic simulation dance must now be supplemented by an enacting of great subjects taken from the myths of creation and settlement. The prototype of all shrine dances is that rather crude belly dance the shaman dance of Uzume, which enticed the sun goddess out of her cave, where she was sulkily hiding.

Every shrine had its own myth and mimed it in dance during the festival. A kerygmatic element is perhaps now added to the motif of giving pleasure to the gods: the performance has to teach the congregation about the shrine myth. But the subject-matter also covered general mythology, the ancient history of the country and the imperial house as well as the fates of ancestors, national heroes and religious leaders. The Japanese feels that divine blood runs in his veins. Close association with gods and ancestral spirits is quite possible to him. The gods are thought of more or less anthropomorphically, in human proportions. They manifest themselves, they speak human language, they suffer human fates and betray human feelings and passions. Mankind can tell the story—that is the original meaning of myth. But what can be spoken by word of mouth can also be represented in the mythical mime-dance, *monomane.* The rites reflect the view of life of a peasant population; in the endless changing of the seasons, in sowing and harvest, they feel the strength of the original forces of creation which still secure their existence and that of their posterity. The worshipper simulates the conditions he is praying for to ensure that they are granted: fruitfulness for men, animals and plants. By imitating the principal auspicious events of myth he creates confidence in the favourable future of his history. The plants' cycle of growth and decay, the passing of the year and of the day,

35

he explains by the legend of the death and re-birth of a god. The disappearance of the sulky sun goddess, for example, is just such a representation of death; the cave signifies the grave. The festival, the ritual mark the intimate closeness between the earthly and the celestial. Their repetition in the yearly cycle ensures the continuance of the cycle of life. The dance in imitation of the myth is helpful to the divine powers, strengthening them in the battle between death and regeneration.

Such myths and dances illustrate how primitive man reacted to his environment. The gods, no less than the legends and plays about their exploits, reflect the primitive man's attitude to life before the birth of rational thought. Since the menacing side of life, represented by demons, *oni,* also plays a significant part in this attitude, it is easy to understand that defensive magic permeates all ritual and plays.

Wilhelm Gundert, who was the first to draw attention to the Shintoistic inheritance of Noh (*Der Shintoismus im japanischen Noh-Drama,* Tokyo 1925), assumes that the old legends were for the most part forgotten, and only still performed in a few local shrines, when the Noh poets brought them back into currency. Much may also have been hidden away in the arcana, so that the theophany of these mystery plays was a revelation in a twofold sense: interpretation of a mystery and parousia of a god.

The legend of the island kingdom's creation by the two first gods is found in *Awaji.* The sun goddess Amaterasu, her sulky disappearance and her fetching back from the cave of death, are described in *Ema, Miwa,* and *Urashima.* Susano-o's battle with the dragon is dramatically represented in *Orochi.* The widespread fable of the snake-bridegroom is found in *Miwa;* this piece, and the similar *Kamo,* accept the union of gods with the daughters of mortals. Foundation legends and local myths include *Enoshima,* from the island of the same name south of Tokyo; *Kuse-no-to* from the base of the Amano-Hashidate peninsula, one of the three most famous landscapes in Japan; *Yawate,* telling of the founding of a shrine to the god of war in Kyoto, and so on.

These god-plays have some archaic features—hieratic severity, a simple, unchanging basic structure—a roughly sketched fable that no longer seeks to lead up to the impressive parousia of the god in the dance, and lacks the lyrical polish and the touching humanity of many later pieces. Yet crystallized in them is what the *matsuri* festival means to the

36

Japanese: that the divine powers are familiar and near, the veil of things is transparent, and mortals will be allowed to see the gods in the festival sun.

The return of the gods: as the festival draws to a close, the gods are reverently invited to withdraw again to their remote dwelling-place. The symbol of worship is taken back to the shrine in a solemn procession and locked in, as in a tabernacle. But the festival still lives on, in the sense of a higher awareness of the nearness of the gods and of mankind's essential kinship with them.

It has already been observed that the three parts of the festival do not belong to the same culture. The calling down and taking leave of the gods is shaman ritual, such as was known to every tribe in northern Asia and was later promoted by the Yamato kingdom. But the entertainment of the gods includes animistic worship, dances and myths of the indigenous subject tribes. The phenomena cannot of course be distinguished so clearly; but the echoes of the shaman rites at any rate are most obvious.

The rites for calling down the gods described above also include the shamanistic ecstasy technique. The object of this is to induce a trance in the actor playing the part of the god. Not only do the gods take their place in the sacred object, they also take possession of the body and character of the priest or actor. He must prepare for their arrival by purification and abstinence. Religious impurity would prevent their appearance. If there is a death in the family of a group of dancers, even today, the whole troupe is kept out of the performance. Strict preparation is required by those taking part in the Noh ritual of *Okina*. This is the oldest piece in the repertory, so ancient that parts of the text are no longer comprehensible. It has formed part of the ceremonies of blessing at the Wakamiya shrine in Nara for 1,300 years. Every Noh troupe has to bring in the new year with it. Wherever anything is being ceremonially opened and prayers are offered for the peace and welfare of the emperor and kingdom, this mystery play has its place. It is a very serious play. Although the performance is not particularly difficult, they say that the actor who plays the part of the 'old man' shortens his life thereby. At one time the actors retired into the dressing room for several days, avoiding contact with other people and only taking certain foods, which they prepared themselves—rice, vegetables, and sea-foods. This custom is called *kessai,* which has the double meaning of abstinence and purification. The Shinto priests also undertake similar practices before the service.

Throughout the country, wherever the religious theatre is still taken seriously, the actors are subject to similar obligations. Mostly they are young men, who are kept apart from the village community for several days before the festival and live in the shrine; they wash ritually in the sea or river and prepare themselves for the descent of the gods by abstinence and prayer. When the Noh actor, in the dressing room before the performance, becomes absorbed in contemplation of his mask, he is carrying out another ecstasy rite. As a result of this contemplation the god that inhabits the mask will take complete possession of him.

Anyone who has ever listened to Ravel's *Bolero* will know how easily drums and trumpets can induce a trance. Endless repetition of the same tune, which marks the first stage of the ritual played on the original shaman instruments, carries the actor away; his consciousness is dulled and the unconscious lies open.

The heavenly journey is one of the most important events of the shamans. When the actor describes how he climbs up a tree into the sky, it becomes so vivid that the drums, made from the wood of the tree, send him into a state of trance with their persistent rhythm and he really experiences the ascent into the heavenly spheres.

We have described how in ancient times the god came down out of the huge trees. From there he could be transferred to various sacred objects: a branch of the holy sakaki tree, a white papery sheaf that looks like an aspergillum and is used for liturgical purposes in the administration of the divine presence; the sceptre of the emperor or priest, which is made of yew-wood; the black pine, iron-hard and indestructible, which was also sacred to the Germans. Finally the fan and the bell-stick can also be used as the seat of the gods. The actor uses these for instance to purify the stage, the audience and the cast, in a special dance. In many god-plays the actor carries a fan or 'feather duster' as an abode for the god. In the moment when he raises it above his head, the god enters into it.

In the play *Okina* the old man's white mask is the abode of the divinity, his material symbol. The actor appears first without a mask, still fully mortal, dressed in white to express his religious purity. The mask itself is brought on in a costly lacquered box, ceremonially elevated, then put on the actor. At that moment he is changed into the god—primeval transformation magic, the basic secret of the theatre, identification with the role, notwithstanding all the reservations of the German schoolmaster Bertolt Brecht. The old man is now the divinity, in the kindly smiling mask *Okina* and his dance is a ceremonial benediction calling down peace and prosperity on emperor and kingdom.

The acting dynasties in Japan, which can claim unbroken family traditions hundreds, maybe thousands, of years old, like to trace their family tree back to the goddess Uzume. The dancing-girl who through her art succeeded in enticing the sun goddess out of her deathly cave, so restoring the progression of the life-cycle—she is the first actress and the first *miko;* with her dance the ritual and the mystery play begins. For that reason the account in the *Kojiki* is worth a close analysis. (The *Kojiki*—literally, 'Chronicle of Antiquity'—is the oldest book there is that gives information about Japanese myths and ancient history. It was compiled at the imperial court about A.D. 712.)

The account exactly reflects shamanistic folklore. The sun goddess Amaterasu was so enraged by some mischief of her brother's that she shut herself into a rocky cave. This made darkness reign over the whole earth, and all kinds of evils ensued. Scholars interpret this as an eclipse of the sun, the death of the goddess, and see in the ritual that follows a sun magic renewed every winter when the sun's rays are at their weakest to restore strength to them.

The gods assembled a *ting* (a meeting of representatives of the clans such as is also found in Mongolian history). They brought a sakaki tree in flower, complete with roots (the tree as abode of the gods, the sacred tree that plays a part in so many Shinto rites); they decorated it with strings of precious stones cut in moon shapes, and with blue and white cloths, and fastened a huge mirror on the middle branches—two of the three imperial treasures that are still honoured today as objects of the greatest holiness. Some gods carried the sacred instruments called *torimono,* others recited magic songs (both aspects of esctasy technique). The goddess Uzume, however, bound her sleeves with tendrils, fastened a fillet round her brow and gathered a bunch of giant bamboo (still commonly used in

39

many sacred dances). Then she turned a barrel upside down and began a stamping dance on it. At that a spirit took possession of her. In her ecstasy she bared her breasts and her genitals. The assembled gods shook with laughter. The sun goddess, overcome with curiosity, was impelled to find out what they were laughing at. She caught sight of her own dazzling countenance reflected in the mirror. That surprised her even more; so she came out of her cave, a magic spell prevented her return, and once more the earth was filled with sunlight.

The stamping dance has a long history in Japan. It is often traced back to origins in the shaman ritual of continental Asia. The group of Japanese dances called *odori,* which form a genetic and formal contrast to the *mai*—circling dances—is derived from it. The basic form seems to have been lifting the feet high, jumping and rapid stamping. It is said to have been used to make contact with the spirits of earth, to appease them. A similar ritual, *chinkonsai,* was carried out to prevent a soul from leaving a body, or to recall the soul of someone who had died, or even to give greater vitality and prolong life. The stamping dance occurs everywhere in Japanese rites, in folk dancing as well as in the art form of dance. It is also found in Bugaku. Every Noh dance ends with a double stamp of the feet beside the *shite* pillar. Stamping is so significant in the Noh dance that the underside of the stage is fitted with resonators, resounding cylinders that vibrate in holes in the ground, picking up and reflecting the shaking of the stage floor. A Noh dance seems dead without this echo. The stage itself acts as a musical instrument; it is a gigantic enlargement of Uzume's upturned barrel. The past is thus ever present in ritual and in art. Uzume is the primal mother of all shamans, priests and actors in the land, her dance the origin of ritual and art. She repeats the sun magic dance in the Noh play *Ema.*

In Shintoism, as in Buddhist-style folk religion, we still find shamanistic possession by a god or ghost. Old women in the volcanic moon-landscape of the Ozore-san, in northern Japan, a real kingdom of the dead with sulphurous craters and hot springs, will give visitors messages from their dead. In the Izumo district they still dance a *kagura* that includes genuine possession of the dancers. Possession and prophecy formed part of the *yudate-kagura* (hot water ritual) until present times. Many so-called modern religions started with mediumistic women. This is particularly true of dance-religions, which secure 'medicine and salvation' for their devotees by means of long, ecstatic dances. Shamanistic practices still crop up everywhere.

It should not surprise us, therefore, that possession is actually the theme of many Noh plays. In the play of *Makiginu,* a *miko* (temple dancing-girl), carrying out her duties in a little temple in Kumano, is seized with frenzy. It seems as if every one of the gods and Buddhas has taken possession of her. She dances about like a madwoman, jumps, stamps, crouches down, swings her sleeves and crushes her rosary in her hands; after a long *kagura* she calms down and returns to consciousness.

The play *Uta-ura* depicts a prophetic priest who is suddenly seized by a divine spirit. His appearance changes as if he no longer belonged to the everyday world. He cries to heaven, falls to the ground, whirls round like the divine wind, swinging his arms so that he drips with sweat, stamping his feet, now crouching down, now stretching upwards, a tool wholly taken over by and reflecting the divine wrath—for what he prophesies in dance and song is the record of the Buddhist hell.

Mask

The mask is an object of worship going back to the remote past. Beings of whom no idols may be made may appear in the mask—gods, ghosts, totem-animals and nature demons. They visit the world of man at holy times, at the turning-points of the year—sowing and harvest, the end and the beginning of the year. The mask carries its wearer away—he may be a priest or shaman, or any other chosen mortal—beyond the confines of earthly existence. The celestial being manifests itself in it. The mask itself becomes the abode, the incarnation of the divinity. The transcendent reaches down through the possession of the human wearer. It is not therefore an instrument of the hidden, but of theophany, radiant or menacing. Yet its terrors are softened by its resemblance to the familiar human countenance.

The Noh actor therefore absorbs himself completely in the contemplation of his mask before he puts it on. Then, fully dressed, he stands in front of the great three-sided mirror and continues his meditation, so that the essence of the foreign being may completely take possession of him. That is why they say that a good mask controls its wearer, and not the other way round. The enchantment that it exercises goes back to the very beginning of the theatre, to total identification with the role, to the ecstatic possession of the shamans.

Noh divides the vast number of supernatural and mortal beings into five categories, the plays being divided into five groups: (1) Shinto gods; (2) man; (3) woman; (4) humans in a crisis; (5) manifestations of demons and Buddhist saviours.

Some eighty masks have been created over the centuries to represent all these different characters. The man is always the actor; he needs the mask when he has to play the part of a woman, a being from the other world, a god or a ghost or a nature-demon. It enables him to exceed the limitations of his corporeal self, to change into an entirely different being. This transforming unity brings about evocation of a distant past,

43

of the life of the underworld, of a radiant transcendence, even revival of the androgynous one-ness of the ancients; with the help of the mask the actor can be at once man and woman, human and god, living and dead. Through its mysterious magic he brings to life a totality accessible in no other way. 'The distant being, perceptible only far off, flows into our presence through the mask' (Kerenyi).

The Western idea of a mask as a rigid, lifeless symbol of the kingdom of the dead is quite inapplicable to the Noh mask; it is full of vitality, sometimes strong, sometimes menacing (demons), sometimes very gentle (woman).

The features of the young woman can reflect a suggestion of melancholy or a light, seductive smile, according to how the light falls on them. The combined arts of the sculptor and the actor bring the mask to life, to an expression of that delicate emotion that is all that the strict code of the samurai permits. The *Ko-omote* mask, for instance, shows a gentle girl's face in the full bloom of youth; a marked dimple, full cheeks, a smile on the red, slightly parted lips, the almond eyes extended at the corners; romantic lovers and the spirits of flowers will wear it. The two halves of the face are asymmetrical, the left betraying a slight coquettishness while the right looks rather shy. One corner of the mouth is lifted a little to give the impression of a slight smile, the other droops rather sadly. The outer parts are painted a little darker so as to make the centre look brighter. The demon, with its grimly compressed lips, has a fearful aspect, but at the same time its eyes express such sorrow over the tortures of passion that we cannot but feel some sympathy with it, a creature that shares with us a common dread of existence. So this art gives beauty even to the ugly; Zeami himself calls for a touch of charm in the acting of daemonic parts, 'as one makes flowers grow on a rock'.

The carvers of the masks probably came originally from among the sculptors of the sacred statues of Buddha; there are also monks and actors among them. Their works are among the finest achievements of plastic art.

HISTORY

Bugaku

The word Bugaku means literally 'dance and music'. It refers to the ceremonial music of the imperial court and the most important Shinto shrines and Buddhist temples in Japan. The word Bugaku is used for the combination of dance and music, while Gagaku, literally 'elegant music', means orchestral music without dancing.

Bugaku includes some traditional Japanese dances that have been in use in worship and at the court for many years, *Atzuma-asobi, Yamato-mai, Gosechi-mai*. But the dance forms seen most are those from the Asian continent, which came to Japan from Korea, Manchuria, China, India and South-east Asia between the seventh and tenth centuries, together with some forms created in the imperial court in Kyoto in the tenth and eleventh centuries.

A counterpart has been preserved on the continent in the Korean *aak*, but otherwise the music of the splendid courts of Asia is silenced and their dances forgotten. The only remaining trail seems to lead to Bali. On the carvings of the Bayon in Angkor Thom, a kilometre (1,100 yards) long, dancers dancers and musicians are shown chiselled in stone, performing their ceremonial court dances; but their art has fallen into oblivion. The Japanese Bugaku is unique in the insight it gives us into the music and dance of the Asian continent from the seventh to the ninth century, a period when the culture of the Chinese and South-east Asian courts shone with a brilliance never equalled in later years.

Confucius himself, in his *Sayings (Lunyü)*, uses the expression Gagaku (in Chinese, *ya-yüeh*) for the elegant music of the aristocracy, in contrast to the music of the common people. The former was used then for worship, while the latter provided entertainment at official banquets. Korean Gagaku is derived from the sacred music, Japanese from the banqueting music, but in the course of more than 1,300 years of refinement and stylization the distinction became blurred. Whether the subject of the dance is said to be the entertainment of officials of the imperial

47

court under the cherry trees or a dionysiac carousal by barbaric warriors drinking saké, what we see and hear is musicians who, by the rhythmic beating of percussion instruments, patiently build up a time pattern and fill it in with a network of notes and rests, while the dancers go through their steps and movements as if they were setting out Buddhist meditation images in the room.

To the Chinese, music was the expression of universal order, the mirror and likeness of cosmic harmony; of the magic power, too, that creates this world order and controls its progress. The five notes stand for the five elements (fire, water, wood, metal, earth), the five points of the compass (including the centre), the five virtues and the five vices, the five colours and the five planets. Everything is arranged in due order, cosmos and ethos, art and religion. The imperial palace, the hall of light, is the centre of the universe. Hofmannsthal makes the emperor of China say:

> At the centre of all things
> Dwell I, the son of heaven...
> To the very heart of this world below
> Resounds the stride of my majesty.

And those emperors understood how to celebrate feasts that rejoiced the heart of man and held the universe on its course. When Yang T'i (A.D. 605–17) celebrated the completion of the great canal joining the Yangtse with the north, he ordered singing and dancing in the silken tents of the palace gardens for fifteen days and nights. The first theatre school was founded in the 'pear garden' under the T'ang dynasty. Its founder, the emperor Hsüan Tsung (712–55), maintained a court orchestra of 700 men. The emperors of the Golden T'ang expanded their rule in all directions and brought dancers and musicians to their court from all the territories they conquered. Thus they were able to preserve the traditions of the nomad dynasty of the northern Wei, who had ruled northern China from 386 to 535 and maintained close links with central Asia. From Turfan and Samarkand, from South-east Asia, Korea and Manchuria, the art of the dance flowed into the court and there was understood and encouraged. Buddhism also brought Indian dancers to China. This was the art that found its way to Japan and survived there.

In 453 a troupe of eighty musicians came from Korea to play at the funeral of the emperor Ingyo. Japan had established a settlement in Korea about that time, so that the best of the continent's culture flowed more and more intensively into the island kingdom. In 612 the Korean Mimashi brought the Buddhist sacred plays of Gagaku from the Chinese Wu kingdom into Nara, and was thereupon given the task of founding the first school of music and dance. As early as 731 imperial officials took over responsibility for the indigenous and exotic arts of dance and music. The Chinese immigrants found a focus in the Shitennoji temple in Osaka, the Koreans in Nara, where their descendants still perform the sacred dance in the temple service.

The imperial court mostly recruited native artists, while supplementing them more and more from the two other groups. When the Todaji temple, with its giant statue of Buddha, was consecrated in 752, the different ensembles competed in brilliant performances before the court and the Buddhist clergy. Some of the masks used on that occasion are still preserved, and so is the entire programme, with the number and names of all who took part.

Under the emperor Nimmyo (810–50) Bugaku was throroughly revised and reorganized. The north Asian tradition from Korea and Manchuria was combined under the name Komagaku. The players enter the stage from the right, dressed predominantly in green. The Chinese, South-east Asian and Indian traditions were given the name Togaku. They came on stage from the left, the more noble side, and their costumes were in shades of red.

There are special instruments associated with each group, and each has its own repertory. Left-hand dances and right-hand dances often have a complementary relationship with one another; they present a similar story or idea or express the same basic thought—or, in a religious context, the same prayers.

The orchestra consists of the following groups of instruments:

LEFT-HAND MUSIC	RIGHT-HAND MUSIC
Wind instruments	*Wind instruments*
Flute (seven holes)	Flute (six holes)
Oboe	Oboe
Bamboo mouth-organ	

String instruments
Lute (four strings)
Zither (thirteen strings)

Percussion	*Percussion*
Giant drum	Giant drum
Gong	Gong
Cylindrical drum	Hour-glass drum
Hanging drum	Hanging drum

The hanging drum is struck on one side with two sticks; the left stroke represents the element of Yin, the the right of Yang, the ancient Chinese view of life, the female and male principles. The same essential duality determines the two keys: *ritsu* the female, *ryo* the male. This Taoist conception even operates in the Noh drum rhythms.

Strings and percussion mark the time of the rhythmic structure, establishing the framework upon which the melodies spun by the flute and oboe are stretched. The melodic line of the two wind instruments is always slightly different. The high, sustained notes of the bamboo mouth-organ (with eleven holes) create a brilliant background for the melody.

What was once a very rich repertory has today shrunk to about fifty works. They are divided into three groups, according to the time they take to perform, and in order of rank. The dances most often staged nowadays take about twenty minutes, but the great works take up to two hours. These last, however, are seldom performed; the method of performing them is a closely guarded secret.

The Confucian ideal was the nobleman who was at once master of the warlike arts, *Wu,* and of the literary arts, *Wen*. This ideal conception is applied to Bugaku if the dances are divided into military, *Bu-no-mai,* and civil, *Bun-no-mai*. The war dancers of course wield swords, halberds, and shields.

In the glorious Heian period, when court culture blossomed in Kyoto as it was never to flower again, it was one of the indispensable requirements of a nobleman to master dance and music. Novels and diaries of the time often record such festivals in the palaces of the nobles, in the temples and shrines, and especially at the imperial court. Bugaku was intimately

50

bound up with the fate of this court culture. When power fell into the hands of the military aristocracy in the northern provinces (the Kamakura period, 1192–1331), the decline of Bugaku began. The new samurai class finally found their appropriate theatrical form in Noh. Bugaku just managed to survive in the three centres of Kyoto, Osaka and Nara and in some religious centres in the country; Ieyasu also formed a group at his new castle in Edo. With the re-establishment of direct imperial rule in 1868 the position of the Bugaku and Gagaku players at the imperial court was strengthened. They came directly under the court ministry. When Western music was introduced, that too was entrusted to the men whose ancestors had dedicated their lives to music and dancing for an uninterrupted period of 1,200 years.

Today this art is still carried on, not only at court but also at the shrines at Ise, Miyajima and Nikko, at the Shitennoji temple in Osaka and the Horyuji temple in Nara and at some smaller places of worship in the country. Amateur ensembles have been formed in Tokyo and in California to learn this ancient art of music and dance.

There used once to be pieces that were performed by women, but nowadays the performers are nearly all men. Two pieces in Ise, *Karyobin (Bird)* and *Köcho (Butterfly)*, are reserved for children. It is only at the coronation ceremony that women may still dance the ancient *Gosechino-mai*.

The Bugaku stage is a platform open on all sides, seven metres (twenty-three feet) square; it is raised about a metre (three feet) above the ground and enclosed by a red-lacquered railing. The black-varnished floor is covered with a green damask carpet.

Gagaku is the oldest orchestra in the world, maintaining into the present day a tradition over 1,300 years old. Bugaku is likewise the oldest mask-theatre. Masks were used for plays from India, South-east Asia and Korea. They are bigger than the masks used in Noh. There is scarcely any connexion between the two forms. Bugaku masks are carved from wood and lacquered, and represent men, dragons and birds. In some pieces they use a paper mask with designs in Indian ink. The dancer without a mask is simply a nobleman or warrior of the Heian period.

Nowadays Gagaku music is beginning to arouse a new interest in lovers of modern music. Young Japanese composers are experimenting with the old instruments, old sounds and rhythms. In 1973, at the consecration of the new shrine in Ise, a new piece of music was performed for the first time, with a newly created dance.

1

Bugaku dances are performed on the birthday of the emperor Meiji in the vast inner court of the Meiji shrine in homage to his divine spirit. The opening dance: *embu*. The black-varnished stage is covered in green damask and surrounded by a red railing. Height: 1.82 m (6 ft); area: 7.28 m² (78 sq.ft).

2

The court orchestra accompanies the Bugaku dances with Gagaku (elegant music); it also sometimes gives concerts by itself. Besides percussion and string instruments it contains three wind instruments: the transverse flute and the *hichiriki* or flageolet with nine holes, which can be seen at the back, and the mouth-operated bamboo organ in the front row.

3

The dancers wear the costumes of the imperial guard and of courtesans of the Heian period. Several layers of clothing are put on over one another so that only a strip of some of them can be seen.

4

The *embu* (shaking of lances) dance opens the ceremony and is used to purify the stage and the audience. First the dancer on the left makes an offering to the god of heaven, then the dancer on the right honours the god of earth; then both do homage to the ancestral spirits.

5

Four warriors, in the uniform of the guards and armed with sabres, lances and shields, execute the right-hand dance, *bairo-hajinraku*. This dance, introduced into Japan by Hindu priests from Vietnam, is mentioned in the eighth century.

6

The right-hand dance, *kitoku*, or high virtue, is probably derived from a Chinese war-dance, if we go by descriptions of military parades, triumphant feasts and banquets. The mask, with its golden eyes and stern expression, is of an Asian rather than Mongolian type. The phoenix helmet may be originally derived from the crest of birds' feathers worn by central Asian shamans.

7

The mouth-organ, *sho*, is made up of seventeen bamboo pipes, fifteen of which have a metal reed. Five or six pipes are played together and their sustained tones make a harmonious background to the melodic line of the flute and oboe.

8

The two giant drums, some 1.8 m (6 ft) in diameter, probably symbolize the original Chinese polarity of Yin and Yang. The one that accompanies the left-hand dances is decorated with the sun and a dragon; that on the right bears the symbols of the moon and the phoenix.

9

The heavy beats of the giant drum mark the rhythm of the dancers and endow them with an extraordinary majesty. The passing of time is indicated by regular beats punctuating a timeless melody.

52

Bugaku

Noh

The principles of the theatre are found only in a very rudimentary form in Bugaku. There are of course some pieces in which the actors play parts, a dancer being identified with some historical or mythical person. We even find imitation of a given action in the actor's performing the same action in presenting a simple fable: a king wins a battle thanks to his terrifying mask, a hero overcomes a poisonous snake and returns to his castle in triumph. But there is no dramatic dialogue, no development of the plot in action and counter-action. Over the centuries Bugaku lost the songs that used to accompany it, and turned into pantomime. It needed a hundred years' development before a fully matured stage drama took over, and the contribution of Bugaku to that was certainly not the most important. Very different forms of popular entertainment had reached Japan from China since the eighth century, known by the general name of Sangaku (Chinese *sanyüeh*). The Rietberg Museum in Zürich owns two tombstones (RCH 102 and 104) from the Han dynasty which give us some idea of what those troupes offered: puppet plays, performing monkeys, jugglers, acrobatic tricks on a pole, tightrope-walking, dancing and music. In course of time theatrical elements were added to this; the actors played specific parts in popular style, in the manner of the Commedia dell'Arte, and put on cabaret-style sketches in which they poked fun especially at persons of note—magistrates, nuns, ladies at court. The few sources we have suggest that this Sarugaku already contained dialogue, monologue, songs and dances. It was at satirical, comic shows of this kind that the townspeople got their entertainment.

The Buddhist temples recognized that such dramatic scenes were an effective medium for bringing their teaching home to the people. Sorcerers, in the forms of Buddhist guardians, *bishamon* or *ryuten,* drove out evil spirits, Amida redeemed poor souls from the pains of hell, and short lessons drove the preaching home. A special sort of puppet play was developed from this, the *sekkyo-bushi* (preaching puppets). Mendicant monks played religious scenes at all the temple festivals. Big temples maintained their own troupes. At the religious feasts that followed the great temple and shrine ceremonies songs, dances and short dramatic scenes were often given to entertain the clergy, who in their turn were expected to bestow long life and happiness by means of powerful spells; that was the function of Ennen-Noh (*ennen* means 'to prolong life'). A Horyuji account of 1341 describes rain magic performed through such a play, which includes a visit to the source of a river, a conflict between eight hermits and the eight rivers of the dragon king, a snail dance, and so on. We find here a rudimentary drama with a prologue, dialogue and a finale in the form of a quick dance, developed from the original rain magic by the addition of Taoist legends.

The sources of material are manifold; they include myths, fables and legends from India, China and Japan. Scenes that show the raising of spirits, the shining appearance of gods and figures from legend, have a dramatic effect. In this epiphany we can already find many of the essential features and material of Noh.

From time immemorial the peasants had had mimetic dances and rites connected with the planting and harvesting of rice. By magic acts of simulation—for instance, by symbolically carrying out the holy marriage—they could ensure the fertility of their fields, their beasts and the families. Here too was the seed of an evolution of drama. The fire god visits the water god—that is, the summer heat on the wet paddy fields brings a rich harvest. In the starry sky the shepherd Altaïr may visit the weaving woman Vega once a year, on a summer night, beyond the Milky Way, and the whole land rejoices in their happy reunion in the Tanabata festival. From such beginnings there grew up the Dengaku dramas (literally, 'rice-field music'); they were particularly valued and encouraged by the regent Hojo Takatori (1316) in Kamakura.

Another line of development to the drama starts from epic recitations. The men of the Middle Ages must have suffered a severe trauma when they learned how the four hundred years of peace between the Taira and Minamoto clans ended and the brilliant court culture collapsed in fire and bloodshed, never to rise again. It must have brought home to them how all earthly glory must pass away. Blind Buddhist mendicant monks wove the episodes of this fratricidal war into rhythmic prose and recited them to the accompaniment of the *biwa* lute. The grave Buddhist concern for the frailty of all earthly things breathes through these tales and, later, Noh chose much of its material from among them.

A further step forward was taken by professional dancing-girls, who appeared from the end of the Heian period onwards, particularly in Nara and Kyoto. They slipped into warriors' clothing and recited ballads composed in strongly rhythmic prose and set to attractive tunes, and danced to them to the sound of drums, flutes and cymbals. They were fond of religious subjects such as tales of the origin of temples and shrines. This ballad-dance was called *kusemai;* Kanami introduced it into Noh. The shrine maidens, *miko,* at the Kasuga shrine in Nara learned their art from these dancing-girls and soon developed it further into drama. The accompaniment consisted of flute, small hand-drum and two cymbals, one of which might be replaced by a bigger drum. Several singing *miko* formed a choir as long ago as 1349. Others appeared in the roles of Okina and his divine companions. After this ceremonial play a little drama was staged about the visit of the court lady and poetess Murasaki Shikibu to her sick daughter. The dying girl recites a farewell poem which so affects the local god by its sorrowful beauty that he restores her to health. A dance of blessing by the flower-decked companion ends the piece. Here too the structure and the style of production looked forward to Noh; the ornamentation of the music was subjected only to one slight change, and there was even a chorus. And in the play itself the beneficent god manifests himself.

Professional troupes came into being for all these forms of theatre in the Middle Ages, and most of them handed down their art to their children. Many were associated with big temples or shrines, where they had to put on performances on the great festivals; for the rest of the time they travelled from place to place giving performances. The five still extant schools of Noh acting, the Kanze, Hosho, Komparu, Kongo and Kita families, all go back to such wandering players. It was they who took the art of the Sarugaku of Yamato province (Nara basin) and evolved from it the fully developed Noh theatre.

By the middle of the fourteenth century Japan was already familiar with a wealth of dramatic performances, performed for the pleasure of high and low, before the huts of the rice farmers, in the palaces of the nobility, in the great religious centres. They were even used to entertain the gods. Dance and song, dialogue and choral singing, farce and theophany, chthonian magic and lyric subtlety lay ready and waiting for the genius that should unite the disparate elements into the great whole. This task fell to two Sarugaku actors from Yamato, Kanze Kanami Kiyotsugu (1333–84) and his son Kanze Zeami Motokiyo (1363–1443). There was already a rich heritage available to them; the courtly and popular forms of play brought from the continent had been developed for six hundred years, and the native traditions, going back to the magic rites of primeval theatre, were even older. Both were professional men of the theatre, who understood their craft as actors, playwrights, composers and choreographers and were able to pick out with a sure hand from the incoherent wealth at their disposal those advances that led to the synthesis of lyrical and dramatic text, music, song and art.

The time hardly seemed to favour such an undertaking. Hojo's regency had fallen in 1333, his capital reduced to ashes; not least because the regent had so fallen under the spell of Dengaku that he spent enormous sums of money on equipping the actors and neglected the business of government. From 1335 on power struggles led to a split in the imperial family, with a northern dynasty, Kyoto, and a southern, Yoshino. The central provinces suffered six years of civil war.

Perhaps it was this very internal confusion that reinforced the need for entertainment. Moreover the great shrines seem to have maintained their position in the general collapse and were in a position to give more employment to the theatre companies. Kanami in fact was given a post at the Kofuku temple and at the Kasuga shrine in Nara in 1368. In the little village of Yusaki, near Nara, he formed his own theatrical company, *za*, and that was the beginning of the Kanze school. His life as a travelling player had taught him what a wide public expected, from the peasants and townsmen to the clergy and the great ones of the land. His style aimed to entertain the audience with realistic performances, and he was quite ready to include comic scenes. Imitation—*monomane*—the credible representation of character (old man, woman, warrior), was the outstanding feature of the Yamato Sarugaku. But the basic idea was not straight realism in the Western sense, but mastery of the symbolic essence of a role. Ten plays in the present-day repertory were written by

70

Kanami, though he clearly must have written more than that. (His son seems to have revised them. People were just as keen then as the Elizabethans on continual new approaches to the old, familiar pieces.) His plays show him to be a skilful dramatist, who understands the effective handling of the impact of action and counter-action (in the *Kayoi Komachi* the ghost of the dead general Fukakusa tries to prevent the redemption of his unfaithful beloved, also long dead). He is a master of dialectical dialogue (in the *Sotoba Komachi* the old beggar woman, once a famous poetess and beauty, engages Zen monks in a discussion of subtle points in Buddhist metaphysics); and skilfully builds up the old, traditional farce of Sarugaku into serious action: in *Jinen Koji* a wandering monk has to perform comic dances to persuade robbers to free a girl they have abducted. Noh gave up a lot of that sort of thing after him. Kanami's untimely death makes itself felt in a loss of theatrical effectiveness, of public appeal. We can of course only appreciate Kanami indirectly, through what his son has written. In a theoretical work called *Kadensho (Handing Down of the Flower),* dated about 1400, he sets down his father's lessons on the art of the theatre. The flower is the aesthetic appeal which the perfect art of the actor expresses through his mastery of technique, through a continually renewed adjustment to the audience's expectations (the actor must see himself through the audience's eyes) and through the mysterious, enigmatic beauty that the contemporary aesthetic called *yugen.* Kanami learned this elegant style of *yugen* from the Omi Sarugaku and aimed at a combination of it with his own realistic style of *monomane.*

His son thinks that Kanami's most important contribution to the structure of the Noh play was the insertion at the climax of the action of the *kusemai*—the ballads, strongly rhythmic, set to charming tunes and accompanied by music and dancing, which were performed with such success by the Shirabyoshi dancing-girls. This was the jazz, the pop music of the time. Kanami learned about it from the dancing-girl Otozuru in Nara. This epic dance forms the climax of most Noh plays to this day. Kanami achieved his great breakthrough in 1369, in the course of a seven-day performance at the Daigoji temple, south of Kyoto. His fame then spread to the capital, so that at his next great appearance, at the Imagumano shrine in Kyoto in 1374, the shogun Yoshimitsu himself attended the performance. The third shogun of the Ashikaga dynasty was only seventeen years old at that time, but he was one of the most important men in Japanese history, endowed with an acute intellect and fine cultural taste. His name stands out in the imperial anthologies as a lyric poet, but he was also expert in Chinese literature and Zen philosophy. He left a lasting monument in the Golden Pavilion, which he used as a residence and where artists and scholars flocked to his academy. But Noh too keeps his memory green, for through his support in the decisive years of its development his fine mind left its mark on the classical drama. He it was, too, who brought the civil war to an end and so created the conditions for the flowering of the arts in Kyoto.

At that formative production Kanami played the divine old man Okina and the eleven-year-old Zeami the rather comic part of the young Senzai, with much lively skipping and shouting. The shogun, impressed by the high standard of his performance, gave his patronage to the new art. He took the boy into his court as a page. With this secure support behind him the father was able to devote himself to the elaboration of his art; he always remained a man of the theatre, but he undertook the first steps in changing the aesthetic taste of the court. He died in 1384 during a tour of the country.

Zeami had to take over direction of the troupe at the age of twenty-one. His name is associated with the change of style that took Noh out of the popular fields and made it almost exclusively a medium of entertainment and moral instruction for the aristocratic warrior class.

The comic material, called *kyogen,* was now assigned to a special class of actors. For a long time these actors played entirely extempore; it was not until later that the texts of some four hundred plays were written down in a language that can be easily understood even today. Two present-day schools are responsible for this heritage.

However, Noh now belonged to the aristocratic warrior class. The samurai forbids the uninhibited expression of emotions, and it was in playing to such a public that Noh became the extremely stylized theatre that nowadays reminds us more of a religious ceremonial than of aesthetic enjoyment. Zeami saw his ideal in the elegant beauty of *yugen*. He did not aim at any imitation of nature, any illusion of actuality, but at a symbolic representation which would be governed by a strict set of rules.

He wished to produce the most profound effects with the most economical use of gesture and action. The hint, the suggestion—these are the principles of the art, which is based on a grammar of symbolic gestures. A drooping of the head accompanied by a raising of the right hand expresses weeping and lamentation, a gentle movement of the sleeves is enough to express the highest fulfilment of love. The whole action takes place in a free land of fantasy; it needs no backdrop. Scenery is likewise only suggested: an oval ring is a boat, a platform stands for a rock, a couple of branches an entire forest. The figures move over the stage like lovely shadows, shining in the glory of their magnificent costumes but only fleetingly embodied in human form. Most plays do in fact deal with the appearance of supernatural beings; gods take shape during the festival in the body of the dancer, Buddhist divinities reveal their redeeming power in momentary flashes of transcendental truth, ghosts are granted brief incarnation to bewail their sorrowful fate, their guilty inability to shed human appetites, the bonds of love or feelings of revenge, which prevent their entry into Nirvana. Only rarely is any present-day action shown on the stage with the sort of dialogue and action we are used to in the Western theatre. In most of the 240 plays that the current repertory comprises there is a conjuring up of the past. Greek tragedy shocks by the fall of the hero, but Noh characters have generally suffered their fate hundreds of years ago; it is simply brought out of the storehouse of oblivion once more in sorrowful memory.

In harmonizing words, music and dance Zeami created an all-embracing work of art that enchants the senses and shocks the spirit with the deepest emotions: admiration of the deeds and the virtues of the hero, sorrow for the evanescence of all earthly things, a thrill of awe before the theophany. Nature is permeated by the divine presence; the spirit of the cherry tree, of the meadow, of the wisteria, of the banana comes forth out of the plant; the god of the river and the mountain appears, celestial beings converse on intimate terms with mortals. The divine is always close to the human; only a thin veil divides the kingdoms.

Manifestation of the supernatural is always shown through the principal actor, called *shite*. He attracts all the attention; he stands unequivocally in the centre. The supporting actor, *waki,* has only the task of asking him questions to keep the action moving, to act as a foil to the *shite*. Zeami does not present two actors as opponents, standing for two conflicting principles: he renounces real dramatic tension.

While the young Zeami was able to sun himself in the favour of the court he was assured of at least two decades of harmonious development. He is said to have learned the elegant style of *yugen* from the Omi actor Doami, the high art of song from the Dengaku master Kia, so that the highest accomplishments of his time were combined in him. Tradition ascribes nearly half the 240 surviving authentic plays to him. That may be an exaggeration; modern scholarship gives us a list of only twenty-five plays that are definitely his; some of those have actually survived in his own handwriting.

The death of Yoshimitsu in 1408 brought an end to Zeami's period in favour. Rivals supplanted him in the favour of the new shogun. The master used this time to revise his theoretical writings, which did not become generally known until the present century. In those twenty-three treatises there speaks the experience of a great actor who had given profound thought to the foundations of his art. Western artists could well learn from this treasury of experience. He also wrote many plays during his involuntary leisure.

Bitter blows of fate followed, above all the death of his beloved son Motomasa, whom he had trained as heir to his secret tradition. He did find a successor, in his son-in-law Komparu Zenchiku, who trusted and helped him in hard times, but at the shogun's order the direction of the school itself had to be handed over to his nephew Onnami, with whom he was openly at odds. Zenchiku became the patriarch of the Komparu school.

At the age of seventy-two Zeami was exiled to the island of Sado. Three years later he was allowed to return to Kyoto, and died there in 1443, one of the greatest theatrical figures of all time, Sophocles and Aristotle in one.

Of the third generation of Noh players, Motomasa wrote six and Zenchiku seventeen of the recognized plays. Zenchiku was also author of numerous theoretical works, which showed a strong leaning towards Buddhism.

The leading creative personality of the next generation was Kojiro, Onnami's seventh son. He only gave his own family the role of *waki* actor, which was not very rewarding. Thirteen of the recognized dramas are by him. Understandably, he put a little more emphasis on the role of the *waki* actor, which restored an enhanced dramatic quality to Noh.

The next generation was the last to see any achievement of lasting value. Kojiro's son Nagatoshi, also a *waki,* continued his father's work with four dramas.

To the generations that followed, the true requirement of their art lay in the faithful reproduction of a form firmly established and now regarded as perfect. Of course there was a slow change of style in the six hundred years' history of Noh. In Zeami's time the tempo of the performance was almost twice as slow as today. Onnami still rode on to the stage in an open-air performance on horseback. (That may explain why Zeami did not like him.) But the general direction of development was away from realistic acting towards a stylized, symbolic manner of presentation governed by a strict ideal of beauty in line with the stoic code of honour of the aristocratic warrior class and expressing their emotions and ideals. Each of the five schools was under an *iemoto,* a grand master, who had absolute control over all the actors and assigned the roles among them as and when each showed himself mature and experienced enough.

Today Noh actors earn their living as teachers of reciting and dancing. More than a million Japanese submit themselves as amateurs to these severe courses, which give them both physical and spiritual training. They then attend the theatres as connoisseurs and, script in hand, follow the actor's every sound and movement, forming the words with their lips and beating time with their finger. Their number is increasing steadily.

This ancient theatre, stamped out to a great pattern by a powerful will, governed by an acute artistic discernment, bears seeds for the future and the chivalry of the Muromachi: period (fourteenth to sixteenth cen-Brecht—dramaturges like Craig, even composers like Britten, have to their surprise found in Noh the realization of those very stylistic forms that they themselves saw as the ideal for a new theatre.

10

The magic of Noh lies in the masks, which take possession of the actor and breathe life and spirit into him. They are kept in valuable brocaded cases.

The masks shown in the illustration, used for instance in the plays *Earthly Spider* or *Stone-that-kills,* are called, from left to right:

Ko-omote: for a young girl aged sixteen to twenty.

Deigan: for a female spirit in limbo, or for spirits of vengeance.

Hannya: for the demon of feminine jealousy.

Heita: for the valiant warrior.

Shikami: for a monster of the animal kingdom.

11

The carving of the masks was developed in the Middle Ages by monks, artists and actors and preserved over the centuries thereafter, mainly as a secret tradition by the Deme family. Nowadays there are about ten Noh mask sculptors; they also colour them and repair them.

12

Ko-omote, the sweet little face, the mask idealizing a young girl sixteen to twenty years old, seductive and easily seduced in the flower of her youth; it is also used for the spirits of flowers, lovers who died in their prime and noble ladies.

13

The bridge leads from the stage to the *gayuka,* the music pavilion, which is used as dressing room and originally represented the home of the divinity in the shrine. A mysterious aura still clings to these places. The front rooms are for the musicians, those at the back are the actors' dressing rooms.

14

The *Waka-onna* mask, representing a young woman, is used only by the Kanze school, for women between twenty and twenty-five years old. The mouth is so made that a slight inclination of the actor's head is enough to turn the smile into a look of melancholy. The costume shown is that of the *shite* for the second part of *Izutsu.*

15

Since the seventeenth century the costumes of Noh have been of an incomparable elegance and magnificence, on account of the perfect woven and embroidered brocades, whose superb colours and bold designs are truly dazzling. There used to be competition between the great lords over the sumptuousness of the costumes they gave to their actors.

16

The actor chooses the costume that fits best with the emphasis he wants to give to his role—that fits, too, with his mask and with the season. The play *Izutsu* takes place in the autumn, so the costume is decorated with that season's flowers.

17

The only scenery on the open stage: the well, surrounded by wild autumn herbs. A mendicant monk, *waki,* is sitting at its edge; the spirit of the dead girl, *shite,* approaches and tells her old love story, accompanying her tale with a dance. The chorus kneels behind the *shite.* The two men in front of the traditional pine tree are also actors; they watch the play, sometimes act as prompters and in case of need could take parts.

18

The bright moon is reflected
in the well of the temple of Narihira.
Beside the spring we once compared our height.
I have grown taller and older since then.

19

Since our days round the well
the years have passed, swift as arrows.
Now, behold, I wear the clothes
of the dead Narihira,

76

and I shall dance again in memory of time past.

20

What do I see?
In my beloved's clothes and finery,
It is not a woman I see, but a man.
It is the face of Narihira.

21

The great prince Genji, hero of the Heian romance *Genji monogatari*, married the daughter of a powerful minister, Aoi no ue. His former mistress Rokujo is consumed with jealousy and hate, which manifest themselves in the form of a demon and strike Aoi with sickness. Conjured up by a sorcerer, the demon appears as a lady of the court wearing the *Deigan* mask with silver eyes. Her outer robe, with a pattern of snake's scales, betrays her wickedness, and she tries to kill her rival with blows of her fan.

22

In the second act the demon appears in the devilish mask *Hannya;* his scaly robe is open, he brandishes his magic club and engages in combat with the sorcerer (left). Prayers overcome the evil, and the demon is calmed (right).
Chorus: As soon as the words of the sutra are heard,
peace takes possession of the evil one's heart.

23

Shojo, or *The God of Wine*. This ancient play of congratulation represents the god of saké with red mask and wig, a richly embroidered Chinese coat, a kimono and trousers.
Fountain of youth is this liquor;
as the moon is reflected in the goblet,
Shojo rises up towards us from the sea.

24

The reeds murmur in a whispering of flutes,
the waves beat like drums.

25

Hagoromo, or *The Robe of Feathers*. The young heavenly maiden, recognizable from the diadem worn by supernatural beings and by her majestic *Zo-onna* mask, finds the feather robe, *choken,* that she had lost, and offers a heavenly dance in thanksgiving. 'I will dance the dance that makes to turn the towers of the moon.'

26

The *kata* or the look that comes from above.
Beyond the mountains of Ashitaka,
beyond the high peak of Fuji,
her apparition takes flight.
It disappears in the celestial clouds.
It is lost to our eyes.

27

The mask *Fukai*, deep well, represents a woman of thirty to forty whose perfect beauty is shattered by a sorrow bordering on madness. It is used in, among others, the plays of Matsukaze, Yuya and Sumidagawa.

Noh

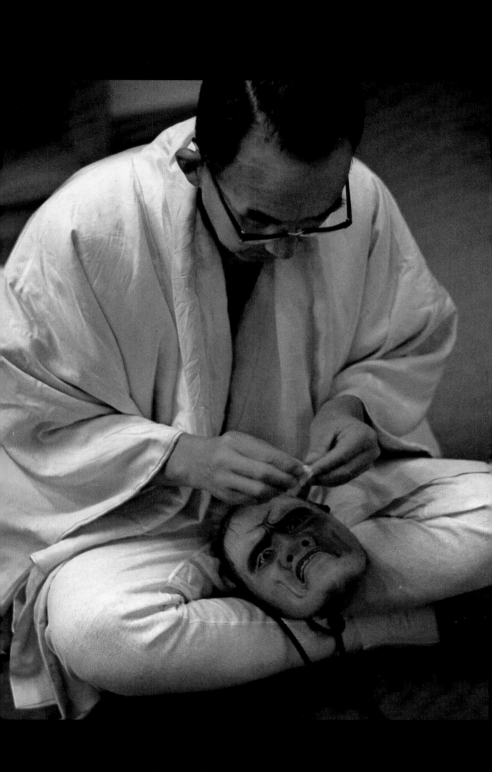

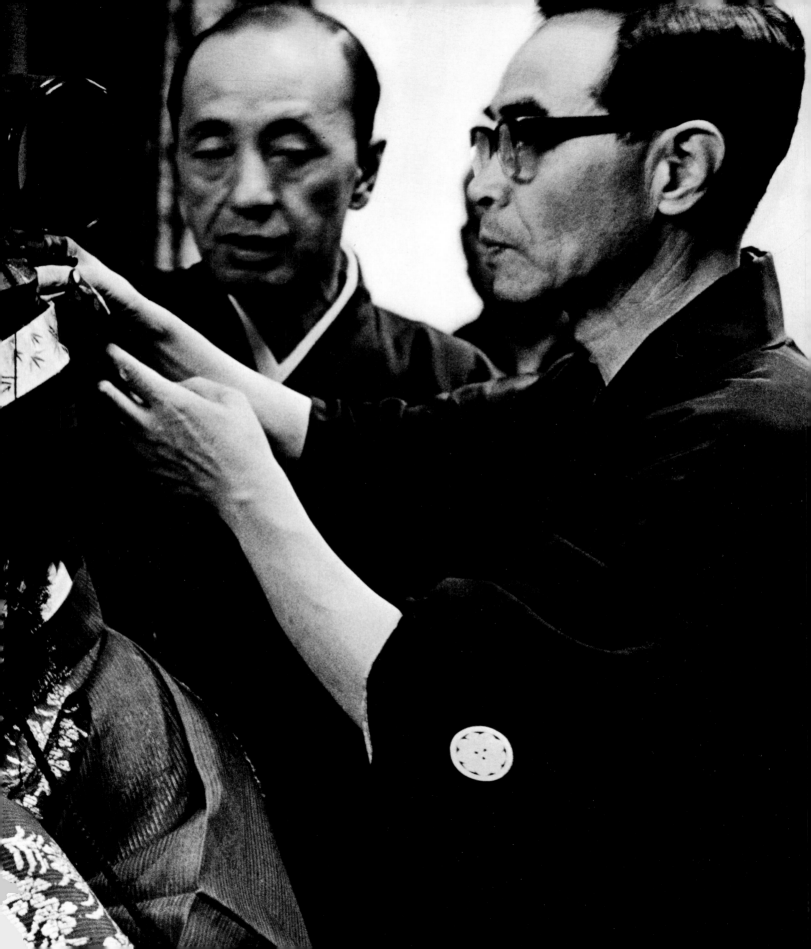

Bunraku

The puppet play and the *Gesamtkunstwerk* of Kabuki were the two theatrical forms developed in the Tokugawa (or Edo) period (1600–1868). They projected a lively picture of the spirit of the age and of the public and private problems of the society of the time. Just as the court culture of the Nara and Heian periods (eighth to twelfth century) and the chivalry of the Muromachi: period (fourteenth to sixteenth century) had created appropriate play forms for themselves in Bugaku and Noh, so now the townsfolk, who had gained in wealth, power and influence in the long period of peace and wanted to see their life-style, their point of view, expressed, transfigured perhaps, on the stage, wished to hold a mirror up to themselves in the new arts of the theatre. Society was strictly divided into four classes: samurai, peasantry, craftsmen and traders. But a man's income did not necessarily correspond with his rank in society, and in the course of the Edo period, with the transition to a money economy, the economic balance often shifted to the disadvantage of the samurai and peasants. Although the traders were at the bottom of the social ladder, they were growing substantially in wealth and influence, while the samurai and the peasantry were getting poorer. Even many of the princes were in debt to the rich merchants of Osaka. This new bourgeoisie, traders and craftsmen, created for itself a new theatre in the sister arts of Bunraku and Kabuki. The two came into being at the same time, for the same public, to meet the same cultural requirements. The important playwright Chikamatsu Monzaemon (1653–1725) wrote for both media. Indeed, something like half the plays in the Kabuki repertory were originally written for the puppet theatre.

The rich townsfolk were longing for a style of production that reflected their own way of living, basically different from the restraint and simplicity that stamped Noh as an expression of the knightly code of honour. Now they wanted to feast their eyes on the vivid colours of the scene-painters, on costumes and scenery, whereas Noh had been content with a lyrical scenery of words. The samurai and the Noh actors who acted for him had to repress all strong emotions and limit themselves to delicately expressive gestures; now it was time to enjoy every emotion without restraint. The painted masks of Kabuki aim at a maximum of expression; the spectator recognizes at the very first glance the blue patterns of the villain, the red of the good hero. Technically, too, the puppets' heads were developed to obtain greater expression. In puppets and actors alike class, calling and age are completely represented by the details of the features and hair style.

Noh is played in an imaginary kingdom in the audience's mind. When, for instance, the chorus recalls in song the pine moor of Miho by the sea (in the play of *The Robe of Feathers*), the battle-field of the civil war or a ruined temple in the mountains, the stage remains completely empty. But the new arts aimed at an illusion of reality: the stone walls of the castle, the red arches of the shrine towers, the golden sliding doors of a palace, the glowing colours of an autumn landscape fill the stage entirely realistically. Yet this is not the flat, grey realism of an Antoine or a Brahm. By means of music and the rhythmic splitting up of speech, by exaggerated gestures and attitudes, by the inclusion of dance interludes, by portraying other-worldly, superhuman exploits, and not least by giving female roles to men or by putting on the plays with puppets, the events on the stage are continually 'alienated'; what gives the townsfolk the illusion of reality is that their own everyday experiences are considered worth representing on the stage. Long before we created urban tragedy or 'kitchen-sink drama' in the West, Chikamatsu was writing contemporary tragedies about the fate of the ordinary man—shocking, not because they questioned the feudal system, but because of an intimacy of human emotion which is not connected with the class barrier but which nevertheless can have a shattering effect on it. The tragedy is mostly built up from the conflict between *giri* and *ninjo*. These two concepts mean something not unlike the duty and inclination that lie behind the tragic dialectic in Schiller's plays, but the opposition is not rooted in a general philosophical position as it is in Schiller, but based on a network of social obligations that arise from the individual's position within the class society. The whole duty of the samurai, for example, demands that he should sacrifice his own child without a moment's hesitation to rescue the son of his lord. In the puppet theatre and in Kabuki such ideas are normally treated with such an excess of human emotion, *ninjo,* that we can discern a hidden critic of the world order of Confucian ethos and the knightly code of honour at work. The meaning of *giri* is not always clear; it can denote duties owed to one's own family, to the social group, to the feudal lord, or it can be nearer to the abstract concept of a Corneille. But those who are swayed by the human emotion alone will find themselves straying over a precipice. In this theatre love and death are closely interlinked. It is perhaps characteristic that the tragic development in the dramas of the period often has to do with money. The transition to a money economy brought severe social and economic tensions, which could be fatal to these merchants, shopkeepers and peasants.

Bunraku and Kabuki, together with the short lyric *haiku,* the realistic situation romance and the coloured woodcut, were the characteristic expression of the new urban culture centred in Osaka, Edo and Kyoto. The predominant style of art was down-to-earth, concerned not with aristocratic refinement but with strong effects and vivid colour. Mankind is at the centre of this wholly secularized world. Even when religious or other-worldly material from the old traditions was used, the other-worldly dimension was lost. In the Noh play *Benkei in the Ship* the ghosts of fallen warriors of the Taira clan appear to destroy their deadly enemy Yoshitsune on his journey through a stormy sea. But they are foiled by the urgent prayer and the magic of the monk Benkei's rosary. In the puppet play and the Kabuki version, a surviving Taira warrior lurks on the shore seeking an opportunity for vengeance. His plot miscarries, and after tearing Benkei's rosary to pieces he commits suicide. The causality of the action here is, psychologically, purely of this world.

The roots of Bunraku, and to a lesser extent also those of Kabuki, go right back to the religious theatre of the Middle Ages, but secularization went further in this urban theatre than in the other forms. It is notable, however, that even these secular forms finally led back to worship, and in many places they are performed in the shrines during the *matsuri* festival as offerings to the gods.

Puppets are mysterious creatures. Basically they consist of trivial things like wood, glue, hair and cloth. They hardly look supernatural when you see them prepared for the play, hanging from a string, their heads drooping like executed felons on the gallows. But the moment the puppet master moves them a magic life flows into those dead limbs. The burly villain stamps around, swinging his hips, in the measureless arrogance of his imagined superiority. In paroxysms of passion a woman seeking vengeance breaks into a wild dance, with whirling sleeves and flying breast. The characters are shaken by uncontrollable sobs, by daemonic laughter; they are struck dumb with sorrow, they stalk in stately majesty. The whole gamut of human emotions is expressed through them, unclouded by any trace of the fortuitous, the all too human, that can still cling to an actor's performance. The puppets give us the pure essence of the emotion. Gordon Craig used to demand that his actors should surrender themselves and just allow themselves to be manipulated by the hand of the producer like 'super-marionettes', and here that ideal is marvellously realized. The manipulator joins in the puppet's dancing movements, he is possessed by the stranger who by some magic enters into both puppet and puppet master.

And these puppets are not subject to the limitations of the living actor; they are not bound by the shackles of physical laws. They can fly through the air, they change their heads in an instant to assume a new appearance. Heads roll—literally—in battle. A villain plucks out his eye and offers it as a pledge of faith to his new lord; skulls are crunched in hand-to-hand fighting. A maiden is so torn by the madness of love for a wandering monk that at a stroke she is turned into a snake. Her clothes become scales, her eyes open to become red-rimmed circles of fire, her pretty mouth assumes a frightful, tooth-baring grimace, two golden horns spring from her hair; and the puppet master does all this with a single movement. Suddenly, before our eyes, a figure grows seven years older. A ghost vanishes into thin air. A rainbow spans a bridge over the gorge, then suddenly fades so that everyone crossing the bridge falls into the abyss. Fairy-tales and myths come alive in the puppet play. The puppet's magic is age-old. The staves that the shamans held in their hands had men's or gods' faces on them, and in north Japan such stick-puppets are still worshipped as divine; old women work magic cures with them. On the island of Shikoku the puppet of the god Ebisu brings good luck and blessing to every house at the New Year. On the Izu peninsula the puppets of the old god Okina and the black Sambaso are taken down to the sea to welcome the new sun. In a village to the north of Tokyo the inhabitants put on a puppet play once a year to entertain the gods at the shrine festival, and after it the puppets are taboo; they are set up in the shrine and worshipped as a symbol of the presence of the deities.

Such was the fascination of the puppets that people tried everywhere to find new ways of increasing their expressive potential. The stick-puppets were joined by marionettes on strings and mechanical puppets manipulated by a complicated system of cogwheels and threads, mounted on tall wagons.

But the great moment for the Japanese puppet play came when, towards the end of the sixteenth century, the puppet players began to collaborate with other artists. Ever since the Middle Ages there had been blind storytellers travelling through the land, telling tragic tales of the rise and fall of the Taira and the Minamoto to the accompaniment of a *biwa* lute. In the sixteenth century another genre became popular, the romantic tale of the love of the youthful hero Yoshitsune for the beautiful pearl-woman, the princess Joruri, and similar romances. The softer notes of the *samisen,* which had been introduced from Okinawa about 1560, were found to go best with this more gentle material. The smith Menukiya Chozaburo, an outstanding narrator and musician, had the idea of enhancing the effect of his narration by having the action illustrated by puppet players from the island of Awaji, near Osaka. That was the beginning of the unique art of Bunraku (literally, literary delight), the comprehensive art-form that takes in storytelling, song, music and the manipulation of puppets. It occurred only ten years before Okuni created the Kabuki dance on the riverbed of Kyoto. Bunraku was forward-looking. A high point was reached about 1685, when the reciter Takemoto Gidayu obtained the playwright Chikamatsu Monzaemon (1653–1725) as his theatre poet. With him the little man took over the stage—the shopman, the trader, the peasant, even the lowly samurai, all of whom were the victims of social evils. This urban tragedy, called *sewamono* was performed mostly in the commercial city of Osaka. Historical drama, *jidaimono,* which had flourished under the aristocracy with great pomp and circumstance, was also entrusted to him, but his heart was really with the little people.

About a hundred years later the technique of puppet performance was perfected when Yoshida Bunzaburo used three manipulators for one puppet. The chief actor controlled the head and right hand, his first assistant the left hand and the second the feet. This gave the puppet greater freedom of movement; it could open its mouth and roll its eyes, raise its eyebrows, carry out complicated movements with its hands. The chief actor bears the full weight of the puppet, some twenty kilos (forty-four lb.), throughout the performance, which may last up to an hour. The puppet may be as much as one third life-size. To enable all three manipulators to move in complete unanimity with the rhythm of the *samisen* they even have to breathe together. Full mastery of puppet technique takes twenty years of training.

The real star, however, is the epic narrator, *gidayu,* who takes his place of honour with the *samisen*-player on a movable platform to the right of the stage. He recites the story of the play in the third person, and also speaks the dialogue in the first person. His voice-control is fantastic; he imitates female speech in the highest falsetto, male in a deep bass. All sentimental emotions are pathetically exaggerated—an intoxicating mental massage. They say it needs nineteen years' practice just to master the different kinds of weeping. He runs through every peak, every depth of human emotion with a virtuosity beside which even the coloratura of an operatic soprano fades into the background; but probably only a Japanese can enjoy his performance from a purely musical point of view.

28
The marionettes are like the Noh masks: the manipulator operates them, but it is just as true to say that they take control of him. The puppets' heads, like the Noh masks, are masterpieces of carving. About thirty of them are used in Bunraku, with a number of variations. They are carved out of *kiri,* the light wood of the paulownia tree.

29
Yokambei, one of the first puppets to be manipulated by three people, made in 1734. It represents a servant or a comic villain. The eyes are abnormally large, and can squint. The features are reduced to

bare essentials so that it can make its effect at a distance.

30

The carving of puppets' heads, like all craftsmen's techniques in Japan, has long remained a secret reserved to certain families. The valuable ancient heads were destroyed, some by the fire at the Osaka theatre in 1926, some during the bombardment in 1945; they had to be reproduced by copying originals found in private homes. They need continual attention—repair of the internal mechanism, painting, wigs—and this they get from special technicians.

31

The marionettes have natural hair. There are fifty different traditional ways of doing the hair, which indicate the character's social position. The puppet's neck is fixed into its head. Male characters' heads are mounted vertically on the rod, which the puppet master holds in his left hand, while the woman's head is slightly bent forward. The mechanism that moves the eyes, eyebrows and mouth is inside the head, which is hollow. The strings visible in the picture are held together in the hand of the chief manipulator.

32/33

The main puppets need three people to operate them. The first moves the head and right arm, and his left arm takes most of the puppet's weight—about 20 kilos (44 lb.)—during the performance. The first assistant works the left arm, the second the feet. Female characters have no feet; their movements are suggested by the skirt of the kimono.

34

The most important woman's head, *Kukeoyama,* represents a woman of mature age, strong, intelligent and passionate, full of tenderness with children, faithful to her husband. Her features express the feudal period's ideal of beauty.

The little hook near the mouth is used to hold up her sleeve or a handkerchief at moments of great sorrow or passion. The picture on the left shows her asleep.

35

Gabu, created in 1802, represents a beautiful young girl. With a single gesture the manipulator can turn her into a demon; her mouth suddenly opens to expose her teeth, her eyes grow red and take on a haggard look, gold horns grow out of her wig. The demon of jealousy has taken possession of her. Compare this with the demon in the Noh play *Aoi no ue.*

36/37

The principal manipulator wears high *geta,* wooden sandals with the soles wrapped in straw to deaden noise. This makes the one who carries the puppet taller than his assistants, who wear flat sandals.

38

The most famous man's head, *Bunshichi,* created in 1718, represents a rough warrior at the prime of life. His expression is that of a brave man, but behind the firmness we can see the presentiment of an early death. These features show the influence of Kabuki make-up.

39

The head *Sasaya* is intended for the part of the pure young maiden or young lover. The gentle expression and small mouth are those of the ideal beauty of the Edo period. Here the hair is dressed in the princely fashion.

40

The stage is very large, to ensure that there is room for the considerable number of manipulators—three for each of the main puppets. The scene is built on three levels. Most of the action takes place on the central part, where there is a screen which partly conceals the manipulators; the marionettes appear above the top of the screen. The lower part is generally for scenery. The manipulators wear black hooded tunics, so that after a few moments the spectators forget them.

41

The princess puppet, *Hime*, in the play *Kuzunohana*. The master manipulator, Kodama, here plays with his face uncovered, but he must none the less remain completely expressionless to avoid attracting attention.

42

Yokambei, the braggart. The marionettes hold the striking attitudes, *mie*, of Kabuki, which arrest the action for a few crucial moments.

43

The epic storyteller—Takemoto Mojidayu in these pictures—is the star of the troupe. He tells the story with an extraordinary pathos and startling mimicry. He speaks all the dialogue, giving wonderful character to the different persons by changing the register and timbre of his voice. The emphatic style of his acting shows how the Bunraku aesthetic contrasts with that of Noh, which will not allow any display of emotion.

44

The storyteller Mojidayu and the *samisen* player Nozawa Kichibei are seated on a stage next to the main stage. Close collaboration between them is essential if the story is to unfold harmoniously. In the language of Bunraku, the *samisen* player is supposed to be the 'wife' of the narrator; he acts as conductor of the orchestra, determining the rhythm of the whole performance and giving the instruments their cues.

45

For certain ceremonial performances, especially of plays of congratulation, the cast is increased to three or four narrators and *samisen* players.

46

Toyotake Wakadayu, who died recently, the tenth bearer of his name, was blind and recited everything by heart. None the less he never failed to pay his ceremonial respect to his book, so insisting on the literary value of the epic recitation, whereas Kabuki attaches no importance to the text. He is wearing here the ceremonial dress of the samurai, *kamishimo*, decorated with a coat of arms that goes back to the seventeenth century.

47–50

These photographs illustrate a new play produced a few years ago for the state television. It is adapted from the Noh play *Ominaeshi (The Woman's Flower)* by Zeami. The flower in question is *patrinia scabiosaefolia*, a yellow flower that blooms in the autumn.

A man and a woman had been living together in the capital for some time. Then, suddenly, the man disappears. Deeply hurt by her broken love affair, the woman looks for him everywhere and finally discovers him at his country house. The servants tell her that he has just been married and is now with his young wife. In despair she throws herself in the river. He tries to save her, but without success. On her tomb the scabious grows that shelters the dead woman's soul. Whenever her lover tries to bend over it, it turns away in scorn. In the end he rejoins her in death.

51

Keisei, the destroyer of castles, represents an *oiran*, a courtesan of the highest rank such as we find in Kabuki. The name refers to the fact that in the Edo period many princes ruined their estates to satisfy the demands of famous geishas.

52

Kuromaku, the black curtain, is the name given to the puppet master, who hides his face under a black hood held in place with strings. The same expression is also used for the leaders of political intrigues.

Bunraku

Kabuki

Kabuki is the actors' theatre. The artist playing the role so dominates the scene that text and author are almost forgotten. For a long time the actors did not use a text, as in the Commedia dell'Arte. They decided what the story would be, but all the dramatic development was extempore. Even when they began to get some of the best material down in writing the text was still only raw material and the actor had to re-work it at every performance. It was not until the Meiji period that books of texts were printed. In this Kabuki is quite different from Bunraku; the puppet play is based on a definite text from the epic tradition that has considerable literary worth; at the start of the performance the narrator ceremonially elevates the book and bows before it. The texts are literary dramas in their own right. The actual Kabuki plays, in contrast, are of value only as a vehicle for the actor on the stage. Taken by themselves, they would often be little more than sentimental repertory plays, empty braggadocio, thrillers and ghost stories. From such third-rate material, however, the passions of the true man of the theatre can take fire. He can step out of the part, engage in conversation with his fans, make flippant comments on current events. Many actors write their own texts. Later it became the custom that authors wrote parts for specific actors, as the great Chikamatsu did for the leading actor of his time, Sakata Tojuro. Sometimes several authors would work on one play. The structure was so loose that it was possible to detach single scenes from the whole play and play them by themselves. That led to the practice of Kabuki-za, in which three or four of the best scenes from quite different plays are sometimes put on; the National Theatre has only quite recently gone back to presenting complete plays, albeit still in shortened form. (Only a few of today's audiences would be prepared to sit through a full-length performance, which could last ten hours or more.)
To write 'Kabuki' nowadays you use the three characters for song, dance and art, and that is a very good description of its nature as a

Gesamtkunstwerk such as might have delighted Wagner himself. But originally the word came from a verb that meant 'bending down' and was used for any extraordinary behaviour that diverged from the accepted norms: *avant-garde* productions, in fact. But even such 'progressive' productions were rooted in the old religious theatre. The shrine-dancer Okuni, who appeared with other women in Kyoto in 1603 to raise alms for the great shrine of Izumo, is credited with the foundation of the new art-form. Her dances in the Kamo river-bed were of the Buddhist *Nembutsu-odori* (Nembutsu dances) type, which were very popular with the masses in those days. Strikingly dressed, swinging bells, beating drums, reciting sutras, all the time calling out the name of Amida, the redeemer, the crowds went round in circles until they were seized by an ecstatic intoxication. These were ancient shaman rites in Buddhist clothing. The object of the ritual was possession by Buddha. Buddhism, an esoteric religion, had taught that god, the world and mankind were no longer distinct but were embraced in the original Buddha Vairocana in inward unity of being, but that the normal man was not conscious of this unity. Its rites, prayers and practices were intended to lead the pious to knowledge of this essential unity, and that was presumably the fundamental concept of the Buddhist sacred dances, which were then spreading like a wave of mass hysteria over a Japan oppressed by civil war.

But Okuni embellished these dances with little dramatic scenes. Dressed as a man, she visited a tea-house, just coming into fashion at that time, and engaged in love-play with the courtesans; or she came on in Portuguese dress with a cross and a rosary round her neck, not of course as an emblem of the faith but because she loved anything that was exotic, fashionable, *avant-garde;* or she mimed the appearance of the ghost of her friend Nagoya Sanzo, who had died shortly before in a brawl. (There she was taking over a Noh convention.) The success of the Okuni Kabuki, in which the ladies were quite ready to sell their charms, called forth a ban by the puritanical Tokugawa government in 1629. But by now the new kind of entertainment had a considerable public, and they were not going to be deprived of their pleasures. So the girls were replaced by boys, presumably from the groups that had been performing dances in the sacred theatre for hundreds of years. (In many shrine festivals it is believed that the gods actually appeared in the form of boys.) But this did not please the government either; boys dressed up as courtesans, exercising their own kind of attraction in fashionable dances and simple scenes of situation comedy, seemed even worse. So in 1651 the boys' Kabuki was also banned. But two years later permission was given for Kabuki to be performed by men, provided there were no licentious songs and dances. The way now lay open for dramatic development. Longer, more complicated plots were worked out from dramatic fable and dialogue. There were various types of role, as there were in the Commedia dell'Arte. For a long time players only acted parts of a given type—indeed, whole families specialized in particular types. What was really remarkable—and still is—was the *onnagata*, the man who plays women's parts all his life and actually becomes such a master of the delicate nuances of feminine life-style that women will even go to the theatre to learn elegant deportment and feminine charm from him.

Edo, that vigorous town in the east where, as the proverb had it, hard-earned money was all spent on the same day, found an outlet for its penchant for the excessive, for exaggerated luxury and swaggering heroics, in the *aragoto* style created by Ichikawa Danjuro I. The word *aragoto* means literally 'wild things'; this style is probably rooted in the worship of the *aragami*, wild gods who acquired a protective function through their defence against evil. With unprecedented bravura Danjuro played the parts of giant heroes who, with monstrous swords, mighty voices and masks contorted with wrath *(kumadori)*, spread fear on all sides as they strode down flowery roads to cut down troupes of villains at a single blow, with superhuman strength. Danjuro reserved the right to perform the eighteen popular pieces in this style for his descendants for all time.

The Kyoto and Osaka style, in contrast, prefers gracious movement, a mood of restfulness, the romantic tone, *wagoto*, in the presentation of everyday life. Many of these plays are put on in the brothel quarter.

By 1680 the first stage of the development of Kabuki was ended. In its second period it came up against the puppet theatre, which had more of a hold over people. So the actors set themselves to learn from the puppets, imitate their style of performance, even borrow their popular plays. Between 1684 and 1695 Chikamatsu himself wrote many plays for the great Tojuro (1647–1709). The puppets were hard taskmasters. Actors who wanted to imitate them had to acquire an almost superhuman physical control of the body. But stage technique too made great steps forward during this period, again perhaps from the need to be able to compete with the fabulous freedom of the puppet play. This was the period that saw the introduction of the revolving stage, the trapdoor and so on.

In all the plays that they took from the puppet repertory they retained the singers and the *samisen* accompaniment. The stage music, however, was considerably elaborated, with a great number of exotic instruments (kettledrum, flute, *samisen,* hand-drum, gong, bells and various percussion instruments), which were placed behind a window next to the stage left. In the later Edo period Kabuki took another step forward, this time of a very dubious kind. The praise of all sorts of evil was sung unashamedly—torture, incest, prostitution, eroticism, sadism indicated the collapsing values of a world on the way to ruin. But once more a gifted playwright rescued the drama, in the person of Kawatake Mokuami.

The Meiji period finally allowed Kabuki to reinforce itself from the Noh repertory. Some great popular plays came from this hitherto inaccessible treasury. The Togukawa had till then kept a jealous eye on Noh, of which they were patrons. In the Kabuki adaptation of Noh plays we find the pine tree on the back wall of the stage; musicians and singers sit in front of it, on the open stage.

New plays are being written in our own century. They dispense with music and dance and with the traditional exaggerated style, and advance the plot with dialogue alone.

53

Kaomise means showing your face. Before a production is prepared, all the actors and assistants assemble for a highly formal discussion. Kabuki has no producer. The master of the troupe, *zagashira,* who is also the leading actor, assigns the roles and undertakes the production.

This picture shows Ichimura Uzaemon, crouching in the centre, acting as producer. It takes only a few days to produce the traditional plays.

54/55

Kakinuki, or writing the parts. Each part is written separately and given to the actor on a scroll, as was done in England in Shakespeare's time. The scene-painters also take part in the discussion.

56

All the female roles in Kabuki are played by male actors, *onnagata,* specialists in an art that has been developed over the centuries to such a degree of grace and elegance that women now come to the theatre to learn refined behaviour. Here we see the famous *onnagata* Onoe Baiko VIII.

57

Each actor makes himself up. The *onnagata* puts on white powder over a base of greasepaint. Only the outer corner of the eye is relieved by a touch of red make-up.

58

The eyebrows are lined either in black Indian ink or in red.

59

A wonderful example of the spectacular scene-changing technique: in the space of three minutes the great gate of the Nanzenji temple in Kyoto, in all its vivid colours, rises from the trapdoor, with the bandit Ishikawa Goemon concealed in its upper galleries.

60

Kabuki is definitely an actors' theatre. Here is Bando Mitsugoro, author and member of the Pen Club.

61

Costume and hair style indicate the precise social position and calling of the character. The Tokugawa government had decreed sumptuary laws about the clothing, ornament and life-style of each class. This actor is wearing the *ryujinmaki* costume, a dragon's robe, intended for a high princely dignitary.

62

Ichikawa Jukai, who died recently, prepares to go on stage in the role of Moritsuna. He was one of the famous Ichikawa dynasty.

63

Most actors are members of family dynasties that have played Kabuki for centuries. Consequently a child grows up knowing that he is to be an actor. This child is patiently waiting to go on stage.

64

A scene in which the heads of executed criminals are displayed occurs frequently in historical pieces, *jidaimono.* A brave vassal generally sacrifices himself for his master, who has been condemned to death. The showing of the head enables the dead man to be identified. The scene calls for extraordinary skill: the actor must display confusion and terror at the prospect of the substitution, hesitation, the decision to make the sacrifice and so save the lord—generally an enemy—as he recognizes the severed head; then consternation at the idea of having betrayed his real master, and so on. The actor's mime must express all these sentiments in a few instants.

Ichikawa Jukai (in *The Camp of Moritsuna*) has to identify the head of his brother, who has been fighting in the enemy ranks. He pretends to recognize it, thus saving his brother but betraying his prince, whom we see observing closely from the back of the stage.

65

Young Koshiro, at the prince's command, is led off by his grandmother to the ceremony of displaying the heads. The prince wants to observe the child's reactions when his father's head is produced. The head that the boy sees is that of someone unknown to him, but grasping the situation immediately he cries out: 'Oh, my father!' and commits *seppuku*. By this sacrifice, *migawari*, he saves his father, since the prince is now convinced of his death.

66

Chushingura, or *The Forty-seven Loyal Samurai*, Act III. This piece, also known under the name of the *History of the Forty-seven Ronins*, is one of the most highly esteemed of all Kabuki plays. It was written in 1748.

In the pine chamber of the imperial palace, as shown by the painting of the sliding doors up stage, Wakasanosuke meets the hateful Moronao, who has done him a serious wrong. He is about to kill him, but the governor throws down his sabre and begs for mercy. 'See, a samurai bows before you and humbly asks you to pardon him.'

67/68

The treacherous villain then infuriates the noble Hangan by sarcastic remarks about the fidelity of his wife.

69

Finally Hangan draws his sabre, well knowing that this is a capital offence within the confines of the imperial palace.

70

Hangan is seized by guards and disarmed. Moronao has escaped with a slight wound on his forehead, but Hangan is condemned to death.

71/72

Chushingura, Act VI. A *michiyuki* scene: this flight along the road by a pair of lovers often ends with a suicide. Kampei and Okaru flee to the country after the confiscation of their lord's castle. The forty-seven samurai disappear and hide to prepare their revenge. This scene is danced to the accompaniment of the *samisen*.

73

The dance interludes are the great moments of Kabuki. *Fujimusume, The Maiden of the Wisteria*, is a pantomime evoking the popular prints, *otsu-e,* once greatly sought after by travellers along the Tokaido, the road between Tokyo and Kyoto.

74

Chushingura, Act IV. Hangan is a prisoner in his home and awaits the sentence of the government with calm and serenity. Under his robe he is already wearing the white dress that stands for death.

75

Actors playing women's roles used to wear women's clothes even in town. In the seventeenth century the famous *onnagata* Yoshizawa Ayame wrote: 'The moment an *onnagata* comes to think he could play male roles just as well when he gets bored with female roles, his career is over. A real woman cannot become a man; it is unthinkable that she should grow tired of being a woman and hope to change her sex. The *onnagata* who found himself thinking like that would never really understand the woman's soul and would be incapable of expressing it.'

76

Chushingura, Act IV. On the orders of the regent Hangan commits ritual suicide, *seppuku* or hara-kiri.

Narrator: He takes off his sabres and his robe. The white clothes appear. All the onlookers are struck with fear.

Hangan: I solemnly promise to suffer death and rebirth as often as may be necessary until I am avenged.

Narrator: The equerry brings the dagger, ready prepared, and places it before his master. Hangan takes off his white robe and calmly sits down. He raises the dagger to his forehead, then turns it against himself. He buries it in his left side, then cuts open his stomach.

77

At the last moment his faithful companion Yuranosuke rushes in, just in time to hear the dying man's last words: 'I bequeath this dagger in my memory. Avenge me!'. The rest of the play describes the revenge of the forty-seven loyal samurai.

78

Kataoka Nizaemon XIII in the role of Moritsuna's enemy, Wada Hyoe. The principal characters make a majestic entrance by the *hanamichi,* the path of flowers, which crosses the hall.

Kabuki

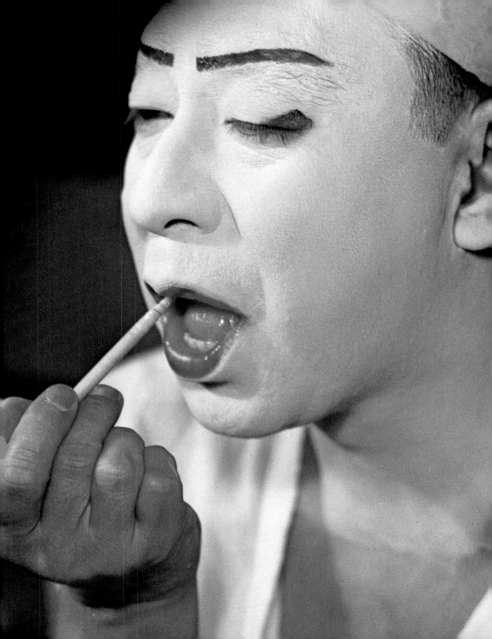

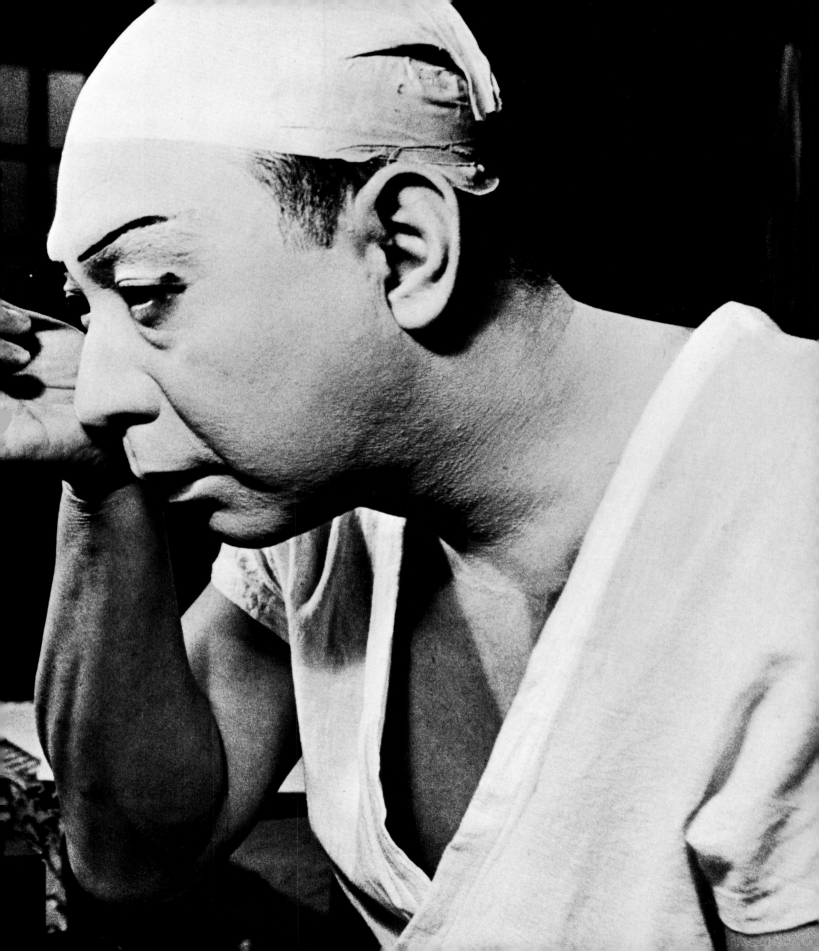

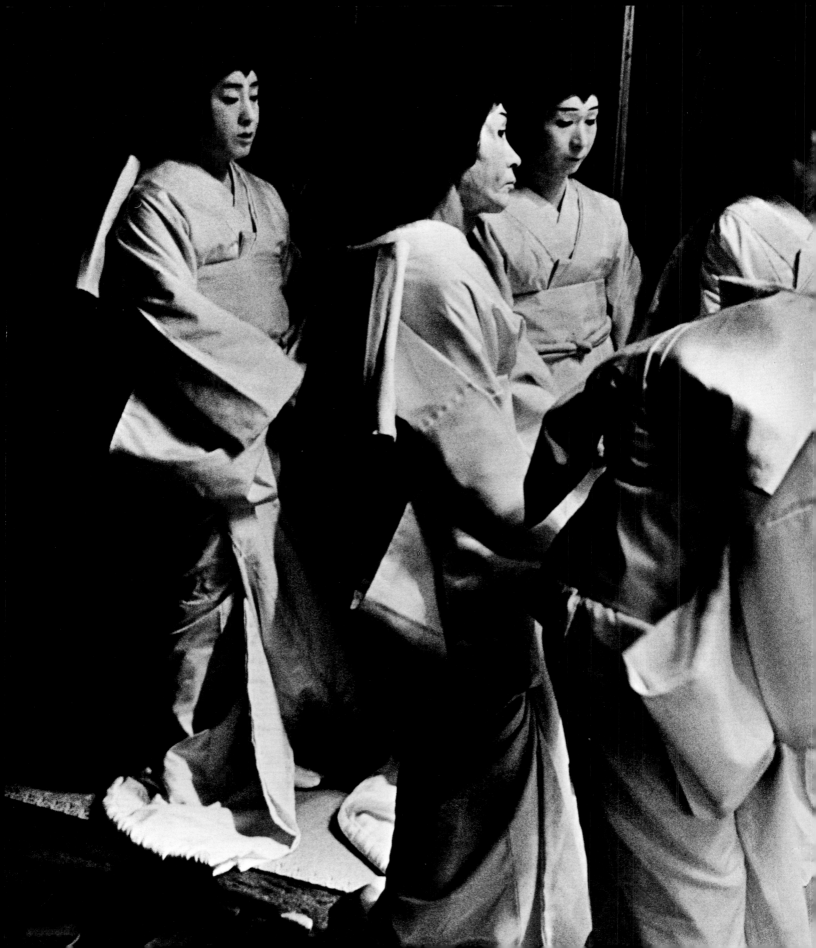

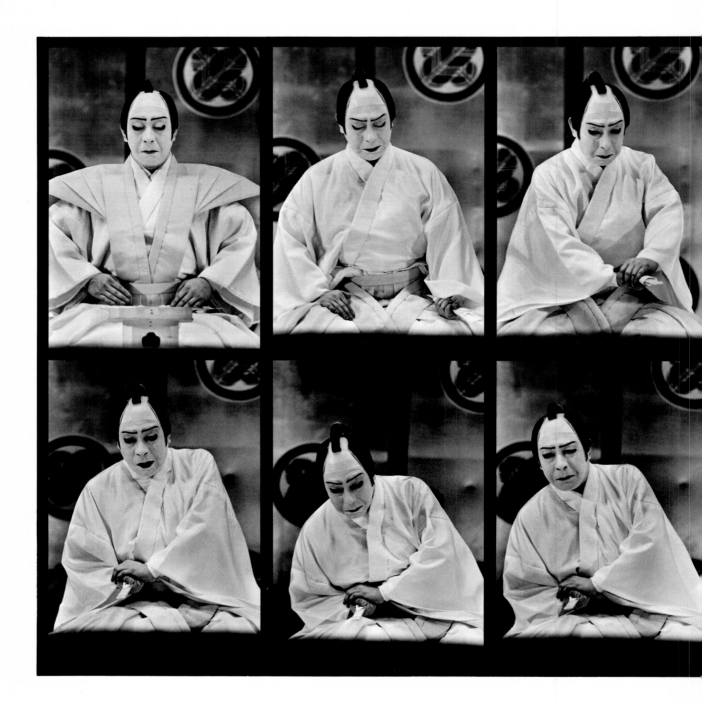

Summary

The aesthetic of the Japanese theatre cultivated standards and styles that are diametrically opposed to one another; but they do correspond to aspects of the Japanese character, which combines in itself such an abundance of contradictions that the foreigner, accustomed to think within the framework of the *Widerspruchsprinzip*, grows more and more puzzled. Contradiction has been elevated here into a principle. According to the title of Ruth Benedict's famous book, 'the chrysanthemum and the sword' are elements that express the Japanese character: flowery gentleness and brutal power-seeking, shy reserve and uninhibited outspokenness.

The style of the sister arts of Bunraku and Kabuki denies the aesthetic principles of Noh. On the one hand there reigns the strict rule of chivalry, suppressing all strong emotion and permitting no more than slight, significant gestures and poetic suggestion; on the other, Kabuki indulges in the unrestrained outpouring of the most vehement emotions, while the puppet play goes in for an almost baroque rhetoric and an ultra-romantic sentimentality in its literary texts. If Noh underplays, the Kabuki actor cannot go far enough in tremendous exaggeration of every gesture. And at the climax of this vivid series of gestures, its progression most carefully worked out, he actually freezes for a moment or two in what is called a *mie*—a dazzling picture that imprints itself on the spectator's retina.

The same fundamental contradiction can be seen in the simple nobility of the unpainted, plain, native forms of the buildings of the Ise shrine and the baroque splendour of colour, the almost tropically luxuriant carving, of the parks at Nikko. There is the same contrast between the ink paintings of the Zen masters, in no more than delicate shades of grey, and the palace paintings of the Kano school with their glowing colours on a gold ground.

The Noh actor droops his head and raises his hand to his eyes to express weeping and lamentation. The *gidayu* breaks out into howling and sobbing over every register of his voice, leaving nothing to the imagination; the emotion is artistically controlled, distilled in its quintessence.

So the hard-won freedom of the middle classes expresses itself in this new style, refusing to be bound by the strict rules of the aristocracy. Here the public can join in—weep with the sorrowing heroine, rage at the sinister villain, revel in the comic scenes, identify with the hero.

Which style should the spectator prefer? Each is perfect in its own way; each gives him enchantment through total theatre. The thousand-year-old theatrical art of the Japanese is keeping alive the expression of different ages, of long-forgotten forms of society and cultural traditions, in a still living, unique synchronism.

When Chikamatsu said: 'Art lies in the tenuous space between existence and appearance', he must surely have been confident that theatre people all round the world would agree.